MY PERFECT PANTRY

MY PERFECT PANTRY

150 EASY RECIPES FROM 50 ESSENTIAL INGREDIENTS

GEOFFREY ZAKARIAN

With Amy Stevenson and Margaret Zakarian
Photographs by Sara Remington

CLARKSON POTTER/PUBLISHERS
NEW YORK

Published in the United States by Clarkson Potter/
Publishers, an imprint of the Crown Publishing
Group, a division of Random House LLC, a Penguin
Random House Company, New York.
www.crownpublishing.com
www.clarksonpotter.com

CLARKSON POTTER is a trademark and POTTER
with colophon is a registered trademark of Random
House LLC.

FOOD NETWORK and associated are trademarks of
Television Food Network, G.P., and are used under
license.

Library of Congress Cataloging-in-Publication Data

Zakarian, Geoffrey.
  My perfect pantry / Geoffrey Zakarian ; with Amy
Stevenson and Margaret
Zakarian ; photographs by Sara Remington.—First
edition.
       pages cm
  Includes index.
I. Cooking. I. Stevenson, Amy. II. Zakarian,
Margaret. III. Title.
  TX714.Z352 2014
  641.5—dc 3
                              2013050636

ISBN 978-0-3853-4566-8
eBook ISBN 978-0-385-34567-5

Printed in China

Book design by Jan Derevjanik
Jacket design by Jan Derevjanik
Jacket photographs: Ben Fink (front),
Sara Remington (back)

10 9 8 7 6 5 4 3 2 1

First Edition

TO MADELINE, ANNA, AND GEORGE,
MAY YOUR PANTRY ALWAYS BE FULL

CONTENTS

A NOTE TO THE HOME COOK

The pantry is the backbone of a kitchen—the place on which every meal hinges. Serving as the tireless workhorse that supports the creation of all dishes and the unsung hero that allows fresh seasonal ingredients to sing, the pantry has a very specific character, size, and even scent in each and every home. No two are alike. But no matter, each pantry is the starting block for any meal. And all starting blocks need a solid foundation.

The landscape of American food is fascinating. I take great national pride in dishes that define our country, such as the hamburger, and am intrigued by regional dishes, such as the chicken wing, that have won coast-to-coast followings. And perhaps most exciting are the dishes that stem from the awe-inspiring weaving of worldwide heritage, blending together into the fabric of American cuisine.

I can remember, as a small boy, peering up into our few pantry shelves in our tiny kitchen in Worcester, Massachusetts. Desperately, I wanted to glimpse the stashed treats up on the tippy top—the out-of-reach hiding spot where my mother kept her homemade goodies. Perfectly lined up on the lower, attainable shelf were the flour, nuts, dried beans, extracts, spices—more mundane items that, at that time, served me no purpose. I had little idea how these could be used to make wondrous combinations. When I was an older, craftier toddler, I climbed up on the countertop, plotting to reach the outer limits, and the aroma when I opened those magnetic-closing doors seemed to seep into my DNA. I couldn't reach the top, but that smell drew me in and has never left me. I was hit with a beautifully scented mixture of what would in essence become my family's daily bread. As I grew and could eventually reach the top, I became more interested in what was on the bottom, mesmerized by how it all melded together in dozens of different ways, so uniquely fruitful each time. I studied the humble habits of my mom and my aunts, who never wasted food and always cooked from scratch.

In my professional career and within my kitchen duties for my family at home, I find that having a well-stocked, well-cared-for pantry makes all the difference in the end result. I have a saying: "I would rather be looking at it than looking for it." I learned this lesson the hard way when I was starting out as a young cook, during a dinner rush with orders flying at me. I simply did not have the crucial items I needed on hand, and from then on, I have always been prepared. You need to have the right ingredients ready to go, so you don't leave yourself scrambling at the last minute. And you don't need a large pantry to have success in the kitchen. When I was growing up, my family had a very small space, and those home-cooked meals in our kitchen were some of the best I have ever eaten.

I have a strong belief in the basics. I like natural ingredients prepared in ways that enhance their inherent flavors. I don't like masking foods or manipulating them so they taste like something completely different. I don't keep an overly stocked refrigerator and freezer, and I try to get to the grocery a few times a week for anything fresh. Then I keep my pantry filled with moderate quantities of the purest ingredients I can get my hands on. You can definitely cook without a refrigerator, but it is nearly impossible to create a meal worth eating without a pantry.

Included in the following pages are fifty essential and basic items that you should stock in your pantry to fuel a range of American meals, morning through night. Each section begins with background and information on the pantry item and finishes up with three corresponding recipes. These recipes are all very doable, even for someone new to cooking, and there is a "yummy" factor to each, giving you 150 choices of approachable, delicious dishes to make. Your pantry should not be intimidating but rather a pillar of support for your efforts in front of the stove.

I have also narrowed down a list of spices you should stock to round out your pantry. The spice aisle is sometimes confusing and overwhelming with its number of choices, varieties, and brands. The Foundation Items section breaks down the information in an easy, comprehensible way and details what you should always keep on hand.

Truly, it gives me great satisfaction to cook in a smart, efficient way using what is on my shelves, and I am excited to share these pantry-focused recipes with you. I hope you will use this book to create and enjoy your own solid, robust pantry from which many meals and memories will grow.

**CHEERS,
GEOFFREY**

FOUNDATION ITEMS

A vast array of spices, spice blends, powders, and oils are widely available, but I have sifted through the lot, selecting those most essential to an American pantry. These staples, although not the centerpiece of any dish, enhance the pantry and play a strong supporting role in the recipes in which they are featured. I suggest stocking up on each of the following items in small quantities and replacing at least once per year.

ALLSPICE

Despite the name, this staple is not a mix of "all" spices but a single product of an evergreen shrub from which small berries are picked, dried, and ground into a fragrant reddish-brown powder. Once dried, the berries look like peppercorns, but instead their flavor has notes of cinnamon, clove, and nutmeg. Mainly exported out of Jamaica, allspice is popular in many regions around the world, including the United States.

BAY LEAVES

Green in color, bay leaves come from the laurel tree, a plant that at one time dominated forested areas of the Mediterranean and that was used in ancient Greece to make the iconic laurel wreaths. The leaves, once picked, are dried and then packaged whole. Extremely aromatic, just one or two leaves are needed to flavor a batch of soup, stew, or sauce. But the leaves should not be eaten, so be sure to remove them from any dish before serving.

CAYENNE PEPPER

The cayenne chile pepper, a red pepper that is dried and ground into a powder, adds a fiery yet tolerable heat to sauces, soups, and meats and is said to boost metabolism. Named for the city of Cayenne in French Guinea and traceable to the Tupi Indians, cayenne pepper has a wide variety of uses, from flavoring dry rubs and marinades to spicing chili. Buy it in small quantities and replace when necessary, because the natural chile essence dissipates quickly.

CELERY SALT

A humble and often overlooked spice, celery salt is unmistakably American. Great in Bloody Marys and lobster rolls, it lends salty depth and a beautiful celery aroma without overshadowing the main ingredients of a dish. As an alternative to buying, you can make this flavored salt on your own: Combine 1 part kosher salt and 1 part celery seeds and then blend in a clean coffee or spice grinder.

CINNAMON, Ground

Ground cinnamon comes from taking "sticks" of rolled dried tree bark and grinding them into a fine powder. The bark is harvested from an evergreen tree in the laurel family, similar in origin to bay leaf; it is native to Sri Lanka. Cinnamon has a mild, sweet tinge and is also known for its distinctive scent.

CLOVES, Whole

Clove hails from the Molucca Islands in eastern Indonesia and is the dried, unopened bud of an evergreen tree in the myrtle family. It is picked from the tree (a labor-intensive process) just when a pink color reaches the top of the bud, and is then laid out to dry. The name comes from the French word for nail, *clou,* as the shape of whole clove actually looks like a small nail. Clove lends a pungent sweet and spicy essence and should be used with moderation.

CREAM OF TARTAR

Cream of tartar, a fine crystalline powder, is made by mixing potassium hydroxide with tartaric acid, a by-product of winemaking. (The tartaric acid adheres to the walls of wine barrels in the form of a white powder during fermentation.) Cream of tartar is used mainly as a stabilizing agent when whipping egg whites or to prevent crystallization when making candy or frosting. And in a pinch, if you're out of baking powder, mix 1 teaspoon baking soda with 2 teaspoons cream of tartar to produce 1 tablespoon baking powder.

CUMIN, Ground

Cumin powder is made when seeds harvested from a plant in the parsley family are dried and ground. Although they are often confused with caraway seeds, cumin seeds have a distinct flavor much different from caraway. Best known for its warm, fragrant aroma with earthy undertones, cumin is often added to chili powders and curries and is commonly found in Mexican, Vietnamese, and Indian cooking. Interestingly, there are references to cumin in the Bible as well as in Egyptian history, and throughout time it has played a role in both the culinary and medical worlds. Today in some Middle Eastern and African countries, it is still common to find cumin set out on tables, similar to how Americans set out salt and pepper.

FENNEL SEEDS

Mainly exported from India, fennel seeds come from the wispy fennel herb plant. All parts of the plant are excellent in cooking—the root, the stalks, the fronds, and of course, the seeds. With a taste similar to anise seed, it imparts hints of licorice on the palate. As the dried seeds age, they gradually turn light gray in color. The dried seeds should have some hint of green, but once they have turned completely gray, they should be replaced.

GARLIC POWDER

OREGANO | Dried

VANILLA EXTRACT

MUSTARD SEEDS

ALLSPICE

BAY LEAVES | Dried

CINNAMON | Ground

BLACK PEPPERCORNS

CELERY SALT

CUMIN | Ground

KOSHER SALT

CLOVES | Whole

THYME | Dried

FENNEL SEEDS

NUTMEG | Ground

CAYENNE PEPPER

SEA SALT

VANILLA BEANS | Whole

CREAM OF TARTAR

GARLIC POWDER

Garlic, part of the onion family, is a white bulb that grows underground and consists of many cloves. To make garlic powder, you simply dry peeled cloves of garlic (in the oven on low heat or in a dehydrator), and when cooled, grind in a clean coffee or spice grinder. Whereas whole raw cloves of garlic are unmistakably sharp in taste, garlic powder offers a less aggressive garlic flavor.

MUSTARD SEEDS

Mustard plants are bright yellow. The unopened blossoms on each stem provide dozens of tiny, spherical seeds that deliver a pungent sinus-awakening kick. For a mustard condiment, you can grind or combine the seeds with water, vinegar, clove, wine, honey, horseradish, tarragon—the possibilities are endless. In my opinion, the French make it best. The whole seeds make an excellent crust on meats, similar to whole peppercorns. In the store, you'll see both black and yellow (also referred to as white) mustard seeds on the spice shelf. The black ones are generally sharper and more pungent, whereas the white ones are a little milder in flavor. When deciding which color to stock at home, it is simply a matter of personal preference.

NUTMEG, Ground

Found on a tropical evergreen tree indigenous to Indonesia, nutmeg, which resembles hard nutlike spheres, can be ground into a powder that bears a delicate yet sweet and spicy essence. When ground nutmeg is sprinkled over hot items, such as coffee or hot chocolate, it releases a wonderful aroma. Preground nutmeg is acceptable, but for a special touch on a finished plate, grate a bit of whole nutmeg using a Microplane for enhanced flavor.

OREGANO, Dried

Oregano, part of the mint family, is an herb with small oval leaves that presents a warm, savory flavor. Easily grown and available year-round, it can be used fresh or dried. Drying oregano enhances and concentrates the natural flavors, making it more effective than fresh oregano when cooking.

PEPPERCORNS, Black

Peppercorns are the dried fruit of a flowering vine. Known for imparting an earthy heat, they perform at their peak when they are first cracked open. Therefore, I highly recommend using only freshly ground pepper when cooking. After cracking, its effectiveness in flavoring a dish or waking up our taste buds starts to diminish right away. If you want a premium peppercorn, or if pepper has a starring role in a dish, look for the type called Tellicherry, which refers to both the region where they are grown and the way they are harvested.

SALT, Kosher

Kosher salt dissolves quickly and is easily crushed because of the thin yet rough walls of each crystal. The qualities of these specific crystals make them perfect for curing meat, a process used to make proteins "kosher," hence the name kosher salt. And these great dissolvable crystals are also what make kosher salt well suited for use in everyday cooking. This is one foundation item that you should keep in larger quantities, as you will go through it quickly.

SALT, Sea

Sea salt is a wonderful finishing salt, as its larger crystals dissolve at a slower pace than other salts. Because sea salts come from various regions, the crystals can have different tastes, colors, and textures depending on where and how they were harvested. A good all-purpose sea salt is Baleine. More expensive or specialty sea salts should be used sparingly and for specific uses.

THYME, Dried

Thyme leaves come from a delicate low shrub indigenous to the south of France and Spain. Often found in herb mixes such as herbes de Provence, thyme bears a minty, lemony flavor and aromatic bouquet, thanks to the plant's mint family lineage. Because it is low-lying, fresh thyme makes an excellent potted herb for your windowsill or terrace.

VANILLA BEANS, Whole

Whole vanilla beans are pods that grow on the flat-leaf vanilla orchid. Indigenous to Mexico, they are now most widely grown and exported from Madagascar, Indonesia, and Tahiti. The leathery outer pod can be split down the middle with the tip of a sharp knife and then opened to expose the inside. With the back of a knife or spoon you can scrape out the precious minuscule seeds nestled in the inner flesh of the pod. The seeds give an incredible sweet, velvety flavor and perfume that is best used for dessert applications, such as syrups and ice creams. A great trick is to put the split and scraped pod into a sealed container with granulated sugar and give it a little shake. You will get vanilla sugar, which can then be used to sweeten hot beverages or when making an apple tart. When purchasing vanilla beans, look for pods that are plump and still pliable, and if you are not using them right away, store them tightly wrapped in a cool, dry place.

VANILLA EXTRACT

Vanilla extract is made by combining vanilla pods with alcohol and letting the mixture steep for two months. It is best to buy a premium brand of extract, as economy brands are stretched with extra alcohol and authentic vanilla may not even be present. I prefer using extract when baking sweet items such as brownies, cookies, or fudge.

50 ESSENTIAL PANTRY INGREDIENTS AND RECIPES

1 ALMONDS
WHOLE

There are many nuts you could stock in your pantry but none as nutritious and delicious as almonds. They are packed with vitamin E, magnesium, and calcium and are low in saturated fat with no cholesterol. Native to the Middle East, almond is both the species name of the tree and the name of the edible nut that grows on the tree.

Almonds are available for purchase in many different forms—whole, whole skinned, slivered, sliced, and sliced without the skins. You can also find them ground into flour, bottled as an extract, and made into marzipan. They all have their own uses, but whole almonds are the most versatile to have around and can be chopped or ground as needed. And because they are less processed, whole almonds with skin will last longer. The taste of an almond is undoubtedly savory, but you can definitely detect a mildly sweet undertone, too.

Tips

- Store in an airtight container to preserve freshness. Keeping them in the refrigerator or freezer will increase their shelf life as well.

- Whole almonds are healthier than skinned because the skin contains beneficial compounds not found in the nut.

- Combine whole almonds, walnuts, and raisins to create an easy wholesome snack—one that I enjoy today as much as I did as a child.

GRILLED SALMON
WITH ALMOND TARRAGON ROMESCO

I am always searching for condiments that deliver maximum flavor using a minimum amount of ingredients. Romesco, traditionally made with almonds and red peppers, fits my criteria perfectly. Here, the whole almonds add earthiness and the piquillo peppers contribute a mild smokiness. Piquillos are available canned in better grocery stores and specialty stores. If you can't find them, you can of course substitute jarred roasted red peppers. Pairing romesco with grilled salmon is a solid match because the nuttiness of the romesco holds up well to the char on the fish.

■ SERVES 4

ROMESCO

½ cup whole almonds, toasted

½ cup fresh basil leaves

½ cup fresh tarragon leaves

½ cup piquillo peppers, drained well

1 garlic clove

¼ cup sherry vinegar

2 tablespoons extra-virgin olive oil

Kosher salt

SALMON

4 skin-on center-cut salmon fillets (each about 6 ounces)

Canola oil

Kosher salt and freshly ground black pepper

1 To make the romesco: In a food processor, combine the almonds, basil, tarragon, piquillos, and garlic. Pulse to make a chunky paste. In a spouted measuring cup, mix together the vinegar and oil, and with the processor running pour it in to make a thick, chunky sauce. Add 1 tablespoon or so of water to adjust the consistency, if necessary. Season with salt to taste.

2 To make the salmon: Heat a grill pan over high heat. Brush the grill pan and salmon with oil. Season the salmon with salt and pepper. Grill, skin side down, until the skin is crispy, and then flip and grill until the salmon is just cooked through, about 4 minutes per side. Serve the salmon with a dollop of romesco on top.

ALMOND-CRUSTED
PORK CHOPS
WITH APPLES

GRILLED SALMON
WITH ALMOND
TARRAGON
ROMESCO

CHOCOLATE
ALMOND BARK

ALMOND-CRUSTED PORK CHOPS
WITH APPLES

My mom always cooked this dish in a heavy cast-iron skillet and every time she heated the pan, it had a fragrance of pure food history. In this recipe, take care to grind the almonds fine enough so they adhere as a crust. ▪ SERVES 4

PORK

¾ cup whole almonds, toasted

¾ cup panko bread crumbs

1 teaspoon finely grated orange zest (reserve the orange)

4 boneless pork chops (each about 8 ounces and 1 inch thick)

Kosher salt and freshly ground black pepper

5 tablespoons Dijon mustard

2 large egg yolks

2 tablespoons extra-virgin olive oil

APPLES

2 tablespoons (¼ stick) unsalted butter

2 large shallots, sliced

2 Golden Delicious apples, peeled, cored, and cut into 1-inch chunks

1 teaspoon chopped fresh rosemary

Kosher salt and freshly ground black pepper

1 teaspoon (packed) light brown sugar

Juice of 1 orange (about ⅓ cup)

½ cup chicken stock

1 Preheat the oven to 400°F.

2 To make the pork chops: In a food processor, pulse the almonds into crumbs. Mix the bread crumbs and almonds in a shallow dish and stir in the orange zest. Season the mixture and the pork chops with salt and pepper. In another dish, mix the mustard and yolks together. Brush the chops with the mustard mixture and dredge all over in the crumbs.

3 Heat a large ovenproof skillet over medium heat and add the oil. When the oil is hot, brown the chops on both sides, about 2 minutes per side. Remove them to a plate.

4 To make the apples: Wipe the skillet and set over medium heat. Melt the butter. Sauté the shallots until wilted, about 3 minutes. Add the apples and toss until they begin to brown, about 3 minutes. Add the rosemary and season with salt and pepper. Add the sugar, orange juice, and stock and bring to a boil. Cook just until the sauce comes together. Put the chops on the apples and bake until the chops are just cooked through, 8 to 10 minutes.

CHOCOLATE ALMOND BARK

The candied-almond component of this recipe is delicious in its own right. You can chop the candied almonds and sprinkle them over ice cream, fold them into cake batters, or add them to crisps or crumbles.

■ MAKES ABOUT 20 PIECES

1 tablespoon unsalted butter, plus more for the baking sheet

½ cup sugar

1½ cups whole almonds, toasted

1 pound bittersweet chocolate, chopped

Sea salt, for sprinkling

1 Butter a baking sheet or use a silicone baking mat (preferred). In a medium saucepan, add the sugar and cook, without stirring but swirling the pan occasionally, over medium heat to make a caramel, about the color of an old penny, about 4 minutes. Remove the pan from the heat and whisk in the butter. Quickly stir in the almonds to coat them with the caramel. Pour the nuts onto the lined baking sheet, spreading to distribute without clumps. Let cool and then break to separate.

2 Bring about 1 inch of water to a simmer in a medium saucepan with a bowl fitted to sit just above the simmering water. Add the chocolate. When the chocolate is melted, remove the bowl from the heat and stir in the cooled almonds. Spread on the same baking sheet in a thin uniform layer. Let set for 5 minutes and then sprinkle with the salt.

3 Chill in the refrigerator until firm, at least 2 hours, and then break into 1- or 2-inch pieces. Store in a cool, dry place, stacked between layers of foil or parchment in an airtight container. The bark will keep, tightly sealed in your pantry, for up to a week.

2 ANCHOVIES

Found in salt water all across the globe, anchovies, known for a pungent and distinct flavor, surprisingly have a mild taste before going through a brining process. Once brined, the fillets develop an intense flavor and then are packaged in either olive oil or salt. "White" anchovies are a bit larger and less pungent as they are pickled in vinegar. There are more than one hundred species of anchovy, and the most common consumed in the United Sates are from the Mediterranean.

Although the gray or red-hued anchovies are perfectly fine, I prefer white anchovies packed in vinegar or oil. I just love them and try to use them whenever I can, especially for blending into a dressing or sauce. To me, anchovies are the original umami, and the dynamic saltiness that they bring to a dish is nearly impossible to achieve with any other combination of ingredients.

Tips

- Once you open a jar or package of anchovies, keep it refrigerated and make sure you keep them covered in olive oil (adding more to the jar if necessary) to prevent them from drying out.

- Rinse salt-packed anchovies well before using.

FRIED ANCHOVIES

Fried anchovies are an excellent garnish on a fish entrée or to serve as an hors d'oeuvre with a simple tartar sauce. ▪ **SERVES 4**

Canola oil, for frying

3 ½ cups rice flour

3 cups chilled sparkling water

¼ teaspoon fine salt, plus more for seasoning

¼ teaspoon smoked paprika

8 ounces white anchovies, in vinegar or oil

1 lemon, halved

Fresh Italian parsley sprigs, for garnish

1 Heat about 4 inches of oil in a large straight-sided pot to 360°F. and then reduce the flame and be sure the temperature stays between 350 and 360°F.

2 While the oil heats, whisk together the flour, sparkling water, salt, and paprika. Be careful not to overwork. The batter should remain lumpy and look almost unmixed.

3 Drain and pat the anchovies very dry with paper towels (otherwise they may spatter while frying). Working in small batches, dredge the anchovies in the batter, letting the excess drip back into the bowl. Drop into the oil and move around gently with a spider. The anchovies should float almost immediately and cook quickly, about 3 minutes per batch. When golden brown, remove to a paper-towel-lined sheet pan and season lightly with salt. Repeat with the remaining anchovies.

4 When all the anchovies are fried, squeeze lemon juice over the top and transfer to a serving bowl or platter. Garnish with the parsley.

CAESAR SALAD WITH WHITE ANCHOVIES

Caesar salad is one of my favorite things to make and eat. The anchovy lends depth to this dish and balances the flavors and textures of other ingredients. Do not be afraid of the egg yolk as long as you are using a high-quality fresh organic egg. The salt, along with the acid in the lemon, essentially "cook" the egg. ■ SERVES 6

2 cups small diced bread cubes from a day-old baguette or French loaf (can leave crust on)

8 to 10 heads baby romaine hearts, washed, dried, leaves separated from stems but not cut

4 white anchovy fillets

4 small garlic cloves

1 teaspoon freshly ground black pepper

1 large organic egg yolk

Juice of 1 lemon (about 3 tablespoons)

1 tablespoon sherry vinegar

2 teaspoons Worcestershire sauce

¾ cup plus 2 tablespoons extra-virgin olive oil

Kosher salt

1 tablespoon minced garlic

½ cup chopped fresh Italian parsley

½ cup freshly grated Pecorino Romano

1 Preheat the oven to 350°F. Spread the bread cubes on a rimmed sheet pan and toast until dried, about 8 minutes.

2 Meanwhile, on a large platter, arrange all of the romaine in a single flat layer with the cut side up. Chill in the refrigerator while you make the dressing and croutons.

3 Put the anchovies, whole garlic, pepper, egg yolk, lemon juice, vinegar, and Worcestershire in a food processor. Process until smooth. With the motor running, add ¾ cup of the oil to make a smooth, emulsified dressing, scraping the sides of the bowl as needed. Season with salt. (If too thick, add 1 or 2 drops of water.)

4 In a large skillet over medium-low heat, heat the remaining 2 tablespoons oil with the minced garlic and toasted bread. Sauté until the bread is crisped and coated with the oil and the garlic fragrant, stirring frequently so it doesn't burn, about 2 minutes. Remove the croutons and toss with the parsley and ¼ cup of the cheese.

5 With a spoon, drizzle the romaine leaves with the anchovy dressing, so it hits all the leaves. Sprinkle on the croutons and the remaining cheese.

CAESAR SALAD
WITH WHITE
ANCHOVIES

FRIED ANCHOVIES

BAGNA CAUDA

BAGNA CAUDA

This traditionally serves as a dip for crudité, but it is equally delicious as a sauce spooned over grilled fish. ▪ **SERVES 6 TO 8**

¼ pound (1 stick) French or other high-fat unsalted butter

½ cup extra-virgin olive oil

12 white anchovies, in vinegar or oil, finely chopped

3 garlic cloves, finely minced

½ teaspoon coarsely ground black pepper

½ teaspoon crushed red pepper flakes

3 tablespoons thinly sliced fresh basil

1 In a medium skillet over low heat, heat the butter with the oil until the butter melts. Then add the anchovies and garlic. Cook and stir until the anchovies dissolve into the butter and oil and the garlic is soft but not brown, about 5 minutes.

2 Remove from the heat, let cool a few minutes, until just warm, and stir in the black pepper, pepper flakes, and basil. Serve with crisp vegetables such as celery, for dipping, or spoon over grilled fish.

BAKING SODA

3

Baking soda, or sodium bicarbonate, is a naturally occurring ingredient derived from ore, most of which is mined in the United States by the Arm & Hammer company. Baking soda's leavening power works by reacting to an acidic ingredient in a dough or batter, such as buttermilk, sour cream, citrus juice, natural cocoa, brown sugar, or molasses, to name a few, and becomes active as soon as it is mixed with liquids, so your doughs and batters will have the most rise if they are baked as soon as they are mixed.

Arm & Hammer has never failed me once as long as it is fresh. Baking soda does not last forever, so keep an eye on the expiration date and keep it well sealed in your pantry.

Tips

- To absorb odors in your refrigerator, place an open box of baking soda inside.

- To test if your baking soda is still fresh, stir I teaspoon into ¼ cup white vinegar. It should bubble furiously; if it doesn't, replace it.

PUMPKIN SEED MUFFINS

These muffins contain both baking soda, to react with the buttermilk and molasses, and baking powder, to give this dense batter topped with weighty pumpkin seeds extra help in rising. Once cooled completely, these muffins keep for a day, but they will freeze well if wrapped individually.

■ **MAKES A DOZEN MUFFINS**

2¼ cups all-purpose flour

1½ teaspoons ground cinnamon

1 teaspoon baking soda

½ teaspoon baking powder

¼ teaspoon freshly grated nutmeg

¼ teaspoon kosher salt

2 large eggs

¾ cup (packed) light brown sugar

¼ cup canola oil

¼ cup molasses

1 teaspoon pure vanilla extract

1 cup canned pumpkin puree

¾ cup buttermilk

⅓ cup raw pumpkin seeds

1 Preheat the oven to 350°F. Line a 12-cup muffin tin with paper liners. Sift together the flour, cinnamon, baking soda, baking powder, nutmeg, and salt. Set aside.

2 In the bowl of an electric mixer fitted with the paddle attachment, beat the eggs and sugar on medium-high speed until light, about 1 minute. Add the oil, molasses, vanilla, and pumpkin and beat until combined. On medium speed, add the flour mixture and buttermilk in 3 additions, alternating with the buttermilk and beginning and ending with the dry ingredients. Mix until just combined, scraping down the bowl once during the final mix.

3 Spoon the batter into the lined muffin cups, dividing evenly. Sprinkle with the pumpkin seeds. Bake until a tester inserted in the center of a muffin comes out clean, about 20 minutes. Cool on a rack. Serve warm or at room temperature.

PARK'S HAM AND BISCUITS

A dear friend from South Carolina shared this family recipe with me. There was always a country ham hanging in his family's pantry, and for winter holiday meals they would serve it thinly sliced over small fresh biscuits. I had the pleasure of trying this hors d'oeuvre at his house and fell in love with its taste and history.

For light and golden biscuits make sure your oven is preheated before you begin making the dough. Then, roll and cut the biscuit dough quickly to get the full reaction from the baking soda. ▪ **MAKES 12 TO 14 BISCUITS**

4 tablespoons (½ stick) cold unsalted butter, cut into pieces

2 tablespoons cold shortening, cut into pieces

2 cups all-purpose flour, plus more for rolling

2½ teaspoons baking powder

1 teaspoon sugar

¾ teaspoon kosher salt

½ teaspoon baking soda

¾ cup chilled buttermilk

Heavy cream or milk, for brushing

8 ounces thinly sliced country ham, for serving

Hot-pepper jelly, for serving

1 Preheat the oven to 450°F. Line a baking sheet with parchment. Put the butter and shortening in a small bowl and freeze while you prepare the dry ingredients.

2 In a food processor, combine the flour, baking powder, sugar, salt, and baking soda. Pulse a few times, just to combine. Scatter the cold butter and shortening pieces on top of the flour and pulse the food processor in short bursts until you have pea-size pieces. Pour the buttermilk over the top and pulse two or three times, just to make a shaggy dough. Don't overprocess.

3 Dump the dough onto a floured work surface and knead once or twice. Pat or roll into a ½-inch-thick square. Dip a 2-inch-round cutter in flour and cut as closely together as possible to get 12 to 14 biscuits. Arrange on the baking sheet without touching. Lightly brush with the cream. Bake until puffed and golden brown all over, until the bottoms are golden, too, 8 to 9 minutes. Remove to a wire cooling rack.

4 Split the warm biscuits and serve with the ham and a dollop of pepper jelly.

PUMPKIN SEED
MUFFINS

PARK'S HAM AND BISCUITS

ALL-PURPOSE
FRITTER

ALL-PURPOSE FRITTER

I use baking soda here to react with the buttermilk, making a light and airy fritter with a slight acidic tang that is a great foil for the sweetness of the vegetables. This well-balanced batter works with most vegetables that can be grated—zucchini and other squash, carrots, sweet potatoes—and with corn kernels. It will even work with grated apples. Just be sure to wring as much liquid as possible out of the grated vegetables or fruit before adding to the batter. Corn does not have to be wrung out; just use as is. ■ SERVES 4 TO 6

Canola oil, for frying

1 cup all-purpose flour

½ cup fine yellow cornmeal

½ teaspoon baking soda

½ teaspoon kosher salt, plus more for seasoning the fritters

⅛ teaspoon cayenne

1 large egg

¾ cup buttermilk

2 cups grated vegetables or apples, wrung dry in a kitchen towel, or corn

¼ cup chopped mixed fresh herbs, such as any combination of basil, chives, cilantro, and Italian parsley

1 In a deep straight-sided skillet, heat 2 inches of oil to 360°F. In a large bowl, whisk together the flour, cornmeal, baking soda, salt, and cayenne.

2 In a large bowl, whisk together the egg and buttermilk. Whisk in the flour mixture until just combined; don't overmix. Fold in the vegetables and herbs.

3 Using a soup spoon, drop a spoonful of batter (about 1 tablespoon) into the hot oil. It's best to fry these in 2 batches so the temperature of the oil doesn't drop too much (keep the oil between 350 and 360°F. while frying). Fry, flipping once, until golden all over and cooked through, about 4 minutes per batch. Drain on paper towels. Season with salt and serve right away.

BARLEY

4

Although barley is a very common cereal grain in the United States, its ancient origins stem from the Fertile Crescent. Eventually making its way to Europe and instituting itself as a mainstay, barley was brought by the earliest settlers to the Americas because it's easy to plant and grow, a wise choice for uncertain territory. Other than use as a grain, barley also became popular for making malt and fermenting for beer.

Barley has a mild, nutty taste and chewy texture that goes with just about anything. I prefer pearl barley, which has some of the hull and some or all of the bran removed.

Tips

- Cook barley as you would pasta, in lots of salted boiling water until tender but still chewy, 30 to 40 minutes, depending on the brand.

- 1 cup of dry barley will yield about 3½ cups cooked.

BARLEY WITH
GREEN TAHINI
VINAIGRETTE

DUCK AND BARLEY SALAD

BEEF BARLEY
BISQUE

BARLEY WITH GREEN TAHINI VINAIGRETTE

The grain size of the barley works well to hold the dressing, whereas with a smaller grain, such as couscous, the dish could become too wet and unbalanced. In a salad dressing, tahini adds a luxe creaminess similar to mayonnaise but imparts a much more dynamic flavor and mouthfeel. Depending on the brand of tahini you use, it may thicken too much when you process it. Keep extra hot water on hand to thin to the consistency of a thick, spoonable dressing. ■ SERVES 4 TO 6

1½ cups pearl barley

Kosher salt

1 medium zucchini, finely diced

¼ cup extra-virgin olive oil

¼ cup tahini, stirred

¼ cup white balsamic vinegar

½ cup chopped scallions, white and green parts

1 small jalapeño, seeded

1 garlic clove

½ cup chopped green olives

2 tablespoons chopped drained capers

½ cup fresh cilantro leaves

1 Cook the barley in a medium pot in plenty of salted water until tender but still chewy, 30 to 40 minutes. Drain and cool. Bring a small pot of salted water to a boil and blanch the zucchini just until it turns bright green, about 30 seconds. Cool in ice water. Drain well and set aside.

2 In a food processor, combine the oil, tahini, vinegar, scallions, jalapeño, and garlic. Process until you have a smooth, thick green dressing. The mixture will thicken to a paste in the food processor. Add about ¼ cup very hot water to thin.

3 In a large bowl, combine the cooked barley and zucchini, the olives, and the capers. Drizzle with the dressing and toss to coat. Mound the salad on a platter and sprinkle with the cilantro. Serve at room temperature.

BEEF BARLEY BISQUE

A half cup of barley might seem small, but it really expands when cooked. Here it adds a chewy element to the stew and helps thicken it at the end. Chunky and warming, this bisque is even more satisfying the next day.

■ **SERVES 6 TO 8**

3 tablespoons extra-virgin olive oil

3 pounds boneless beef chuck, cut into 1-inch cubes

4 ounces pancetta, cut into ½-inch pieces

1 medium carrot, chopped (about ½ cup)

2 celery stalks, chopped (about ½ cup)

1 small leek (white and light green parts), well rinsed and sliced (about ½ cup)

1 medium onion, chopped (about 1 cup)

4 large garlic cloves, finely chopped

2 sprigs fresh Italian parsley

2 sprigs fresh rosemary

2 sprigs fresh thyme

Zest of 1 lemon, removed with a vegetable peeler

Zest of 1 orange, removed with a vegetable peeler

2 cinnamon sticks

2 dried bay leaves

2 cups dry white wine

1 28-ounce can San Marzano tomatoes with juice, crushed by hand

3 cups chicken stock

½ teaspoon ground allspice

Kosher salt and freshly ground black pepper

½ cup pearl barley

1 tablespoon unsalted butter

1 cup crustless small diced bread cubes from a day-old country loaf

2 tablespoons chopped fresh Italian parsley

1 Heat a large Dutch oven over medium-high heat. Add the oil. When the oil is hot, brown the beef in batches on all sides, removing to a plate as the pieces are browned. (Don't salt the meat yet, as you won't obtain a proper sear.)

2 When all the beef is removed, add the pancetta and cook just to render the fat, about 4 minutes. Add the carrot, celery, leek, onion, and half the garlic. Cover the pot and sweat the vegetables over medium heat until the onion and leek are tender, about 10 minutes.

3 Meanwhile, tie the whole sprigs of parsley, rosemary, and thyme and the lemon zest, orange zest, cinnamon sticks, and bay leaves into a sachet in cheesecloth. Once the vegetables are sweated, pour in the wine and raise the heat to high to reduce the wine by half. Add the sachet, the tomatoes, stock, and allspice. Bring to a simmer and season with salt and pepper. Return the beef to the pot, cover, and simmer, stirring occasionally, until the beef is tender but the sauce is still soupy, about 2 hours.

4 Meanwhile, in a medium saucepan, cook the barley in plenty of salted water until tender but still chewy, 30 to 40 minutes. Drain well. In a small skillet, melt the butter over low heat. Add the bread cubes and cook, tossing, until crisp and browned, 8 to 10 minutes. In a small bowl, stir together the remaining garlic and the chopped parsley.

5 When the meat is tender, add the cooked barley and simmer to blend the flavors, about 15 minutes. Discard the sachet. To serve, ladle into bowls and top each serving with some of the garlic-parsley mixture and croutons.

DUCK AND BARLEY SALAD

Today many barley applications are focused on soup, but in my Armenian household, I was often served barley as a more dynamic part of a meal. I carry this notion with me today. Here, in this salad, you can appreciate the nutty texture of the grain. Paired with the duck, it makes a wonderful one-plate daytime meal. ■ SERVES 4 TO 6

2 boneless, skin-on duck breasts (1¼ to 1½ pounds total)

Kosher salt and freshly ground black pepper

1 cup pearl barley

¼ cup white wine vinegar

½ cup extra-virgin olive oil

1 teaspoon tamarind paste (optional but nice)

2 Persian or other small seedless cucumbers, chopped (about 1½ cups)

½ cup chopped scallions, white and green parts

2 small shallots, finely chopped

1 tablespoon chopped fresh tarragon

1 ripe mango, peeled, pitted, and chopped into ½-inch pieces

1 The day before you prepare the salad, season the duck with salt and pepper and let rest in the refrigerator overnight. Remove the duck from the refrigerator about 1 hour before you're ready to cook it.

2 Cook the barley in plenty of salted water until tender but still chewy, 30 to 40 minutes. Drain and cool.

3 Heat a cast-iron skillet over low heat. Add the duck, skin side down, and slowly cook, without turning, to render the fat and crisp the skin, 15 to 20 minutes for medium rare. Flip the duck to a plate, skin side up, and let rest while you prepare the salad.

4 In a medium bowl, whisk together the vinegar, oil, and tamarind paste (if using) and season with salt. In a large bowl, toss the cooked barley, cucumbers, scallions, shallots, and tarragon with enough dressing to coat. Season with salt.

5 Spread the barley salad onto a large serving platter. Thinly slice the duck breast and arrange on top. Sprinkle the mango on top and drizzle with the remaining dressing.

BBQ SAUCE

5

Ingredients vary widely in BBQ sauce, and although its birthplace and origin are unclear, it is uncontested as an American staple. Originally, butter, vinegar, and dry spices played a role; they were used to preserve and mask game meats that were starting to spoil. But, moving into the condiment world and away from preserving, modern versions have distinctive regional ingredients and flavor profiles, ranging from spicy mustard heat, to a peppery vinegar (most historic), and then swinging more toward sweet smoky molasses.

I am a BBQ sauce junky. I have tried every sauce I can get my hands on and have decided to forge a new trail. My own Foolproof BBQ Sauce (page 288) uses interesting ingredients such as fish sauce and more Worcestershire and vinegar than usual, but I believe the result is both perfectly balanced and finger-licking good. If you do not have time to make it from scratch, a store-bought brand can work in any of these recipes; just be sure to check for quality ingredients and not too much sugar.

Tips

- BBQ sauce can be used as a marinade as well as for a condiment once your meat is cooked. It works well with pork, chicken, or ribs.

- If buying a ready-made bottled sauce, don't be shy. Buy a few so you can learn which regional style is your preference.

- Opened or freshly made BBQ sauce should be refrigerated.

- A homemade batch makes a great gift!

MARINATED FLANK STEAK
WITH MASHED SWEET POTATOES

Keep an eye on the flank steak while grilling and do not let the heat go past medium high. The BBQ sauce should caramelize the outside of the steak and make a sweet, smoky crust without burning. The steak can also be seared in a regular cast-iron pan over medium to medium-high heat and the cooking time will be about the same. ■ **SERVES 4 TO 6**

FLANK STEAK

1 cup Foolproof **BBQ** Sauce (page 288)

½ cup chopped fresh Italian parsley

2 tablespoons sherry vinegar

1 tablespoon soy sauce

2 teaspoons dried oregano

2 teaspoons dried rosemary

2 teaspoons dried thyme

2 garlic cloves, chopped

¼ cup extra-virgin olive oil, plus more for brushing the grill pan

1 flank steak (1¾ to 2 pounds)

Kosher salt and freshly ground black pepper

½ cup chopped fresh chives (optional)

SWEET POTATOES

3 medium sweet potatoes, peeled and cut into 2-inch chunks, about 2½ pounds

Kosher salt

4 tablespoons (½ stick) unsalted butter, cut in chunks

2 tablespoons pure maple syrup

2 tablespoons orange juice concentrate, thawed

½ teaspoon ground cinnamon

Freshly ground black pepper

1 To make the flank steak: In a large baking dish, whisk together the BBQ sauce, parsley, vinegar, soy sauce, oregano, rosemary, thyme, and garlic. Whisk in the oil to combine. Dredge the steak on both sides in the marinade, cover with plastic wrap, and refrigerate at least 8 hours or overnight.

2 Remove the steak from the refrigerator 30 minutes before you're ready to cook and preheat a grill or grill pan to medium high.

3 To make the sweet potatoes: Put the potatoes in salted water to cover by 2 inches. Bring to a simmer and cook until tender, about 15 minutes. Drain well. Return them to the pot over very low heat and mash with the butter, syrup, orange juice concentrate, cinnamon, and salt and pepper to taste. Keep the sweet potatoes warm while you grill the steak.

4 Remove the steak from the marinade and pat dry. Season with salt and pepper. Brush the grill or grill pan with a little oil. Grill the steak on both sides until caramelized and cooked to your liking, 4 to 5 minutes per side for medium rare. Let sit at room temperature for 10 minutes and then slice against the grain into thin slices. Serve on top of the sweet potatoes, garnishing each serving with a sprinkling of chopped chives, if desired.

SUPERCHARGED
CHICKEN WINGS

CAST-IRON
BURGERS WITH
SECRET SAUCE

MARINATED
FLANK STEAK WITH
MASHED SWEET
POTATOES

SUPERCHARGED CHICKEN WINGS

I like to serve these on a leisurely Sunday afternoon when there is no set "meal time" and friends or family are stopping by. The obvious choice is to make these for watching football, but I like a hearty batch when watching a golf tournament, too. The nontraditional use of BBQ sauce in preparing these wings adds a smoky richness to the meat that is not found when simply coating the wings in a traditional hot sauce. ■ SERVES 4

¼ pound (1 stick) unsalted butter, softened

6 ounces Roquefort or other blue cheese, crumbled

½ cup Foolproof BBQ Sauce (page 288) or store-bought

½ cup piquillo peppers, drained well

2 teaspoons ground cumin

2 teaspoons smoked paprika

Canola oil, for frying

1 cup all-purpose flour

Kosher salt and freshly ground black pepper

2½ pounds chicken wings, separated at the joints and patted dry

1 In a medium bowl, whisk together the butter and 4 ounces of the blue cheese to make a smooth, soft butter. Transfer to a serving bowl and set aside at room temperature (you want this to remain creamy but not melted).

2 In a blender, puree the BBQ sauce, piquillos, 1 teaspoon cumin, and 1 teaspoon paprika. Pour into a bowl large enough to hold the wings once fried.

3 In a deep pot, heat 3 inches of oil to 365°F. In a shallow dish, combine the flour with the remaining 1 teaspoon cumin and paprika, and season with salt and pepper. Then season the wings with salt and pepper. Dredge them lightly in the flour and fry, in batches, until golden brown and crispy, about 13 minutes. Drain briefly on paper towels, but add, while still very hot, to the BBQ mixture. Toss to coat all the wings in the sauce and transfer to a serving platter.

4 Dollop a little of the blue cheese butter on top to let melt. Serve the rest in a bowl on the side, and garnish with the remaining crumbled blue cheese.

CAST-IRON BURGERS
WITH SECRET SAUCE

The "secret sauce" strikes the perfect balance of sweet, spicy, and creamy. The application here for a burger is perfect, but it is also great on a turkey sandwich or with leftover cold roasted chicken or pork. ▪ **SERVES 6**

SECRET SAUCE

2 tablespoons Foolproof BBQ Sauce (page 288)

2 tablespoons Dijon mustard

2 tablespoons prepared horseradish, drained

2 tablespoons ketchup

2 tablespoons mayonnaise

Freshly ground black pepper

BURGERS

2¼ pounds ground beef chuck, medium grind

Kosher salt and freshly ground black pepper

Canola oil, for the pan

6 English muffins, split, toasted, and lightly buttered

1 large ripe beefsteak tomato, cut into 6 slices

1 To make the secret sauce: In a small bowl, stir together the BBQ sauce, mustard, horseradish, ketchup, and mayonnaise. Season with pepper and then cover and chill until ready to use.

2 To make the burgers, gently form the chuck into 6 patties, about 1 inch thick. Season the outsides liberally with salt and pepper.

3 Set a cast-iron skillet over medium-high heat and let heat for 1 minute. Add a drizzle of oil. As soon as the oil begins to smoke, add the burgers. Let cook undisturbed until well charred, 3 to 4 minutes. Flip and char the other sides, about 7 minutes total for medium-rare burgers.

4 To serve, place a tomato slice on each of the English muffin bottoms and top each with a burger and some of the sauce. Add the muffin tops and serve immediately.

BEANS
BLACK, CANNED

6

Black beans, also sometimes called black turtle beans, have a mild but meaty, earthy flavor. As a standard common bean, they have success growing in many regions and are known widely for their use in Latin and Mexican cuisine.

They hold their shape when heat is applied, so even the canned variety can be cooked for long periods of time in soups and stews without falling apart. They are especially tasty with bacon, ham hocks, chipotles, smoked paprika, or other smoky ingredients. Some consider black beans to sit low in the food hierarchy, but I hold them in high regard. I've even been known to pair black beans with black truffles!

Tips

- As with all canned beans, choose a brand you trust. (Goya and Progresso are always reliable, but I prefer Eden Organics because the can liners are BPA-free.)

- Check the sodium content on the can label. Compare brands and be sure what you buy is not too high!

- Rinse and drain well before using in any recipe.

SMOKY
BLACK BEAN
BISQUE

HUEVOS RANCHEROS

ROASTED
BLACK BEAN STEW
WITH GRILLED
RADICCHIO

SMOKY BLACK BEAN BISQUE

This recipe showcases how black beans can hold and carry added flavors. The chipotle and corn, classic partners with black beans, take it all up a notch. Depending on your preference, it can be served chunky or smooth. The sweet and smoky flavors will be more intense if served pureed, but either way, it is delicious. If pureeing, have a little extra hot water or stock on hand to thin the soup to the consistency you like. ■ SERVES 4 TO 6

2 tablespoons extra-virgin olive oil

½ cup chopped carrot

½ cup fresh or frozen corn kernels (if fresh, from about 1 ear of corn)

½ cup chopped onion

Kosher salt

2 garlic cloves, finely chopped

2 teaspoons chili powder

1 teaspoon ground cumin

2 15-ounce cans black beans, rinsed and drained

1 canned chipotle pepper in adobo sauce, chopped, plus 2 tablespoons adobo sauce

1 quart hot vegetable or chicken stock

2 tablespoons fresh lime juice

Fresh cilantro leaves, for garnish

Sour cream, for garnish

1 In a large saucepan, heat the oil over medium heat. Add the carrot, corn, and onion and cook until the vegetables begin to soften, about 8 minutes. Season with salt.

2 Add the garlic, chili powder, and cumin and cook until the spices are fragrant, about 1 minute. Add the beans and chipotle and sauce and stir just to combine. Pour in the stock and 1 cup water. Bring to a simmer and cook until thick and creamy, 35 to 40 minutes.

3 Stir in the lime juice and season with salt, if necessary. Puree the hot soup with a hand blender, if desired, or leave chunky. Serve in soup bowls with the cilantro and a dollop of sour cream.

HUEVOS RANCHEROS

Huevos rancheros are a fun way to mix up the traditional eggs for breakfast or brunch (and are also an inexpensive family dinner!). Even though there are a lot of components, the bean sauce can be made ahead and rewarmed with a little extra stock or water, and the green sauce can also be made one to two hours ahead, covered, and chilled until ready to use. ■ SERVES 4

BLACK BEAN SAUCE

2 tablespoons extra-virgin olive oil

½ cup thinly sliced onion

1 jalapeño, seeded and thinly sliced

2 garlic cloves, chopped

1 15-ounce can black beans, drained and rinsed

1 cup vegetable or chicken stock

2 tablespoons fresh lime juice

Green Tabasco sauce

Kosher salt

½ cup roughly chopped fresh cilantro

GREEN SAUCE

1 ripe avocado, pitted, peeled, and diced

4 medium tomatillos, husked, rinsed, cored, and chopped (about ½ cup)

¼ cup roughly chopped fresh cilantro

2 tablespoons finely chopped red onion

1 tablespoon finely chopped seeded jalapeño

1 tablespoon fresh lime juice

Kosher salt

ASSEMBLY

Canola oil, for frying the tortillas and eggs

4 corn tortillas

Kosher salt

4 large eggs

4 ounces crumbled queso fresco

Lime wedges, for serving

1 To make the black bean sauce: Heat a medium skillet over medium heat. Add the oil. When the oil is hot, add the onion and jalapeño and cook until the onion is softened, about 8 minutes. Add the garlic, beans, and stock. Bring to a simmer and cook until the liquid is reduced by about half and the sauce is flavorful, about 15 minutes, mashing the beans a little with the back of a wooden spoon to thicken the sauce. Stir in the lime juice and Tabasco and salt to taste. Keep warm, stirring in the cilantro just before serving.

2 To make the green sauce: Combine the avocado, tomatillos, cilantro, onion, jalapeño, and lime juice. Mash with a fork to break up the avocado into smaller pieces and make a chunky, thick sauce. Season with salt, and cover and chill until ready to use.

3 When ready to serve, heat ½ inch oil in a skillet over medium-high heat. When the oil is hot (about 365°F.), fry 2 tortillas at a time until crispy, turning once, 1 to 2 minutes total. Drain on paper towels and season with salt.

4 Heat a large nonstick skillet over medium-high heat and film the bottom with oil. Carefully break in the eggs and cook until the yolks are done to your liking, 2 to 3 minutes for sunny-side-up eggs with still-runny yolks.

5 To serve, put a fried tortilla on each plate. Top with the beans, then a cooked egg, then the green sauce. Sprinkle with the queso fresco and serve with a lime wedge.

ROASTED BLACK BEAN STEW
WITH GRILLED RADICCHIO

This dish is the perfect example of thinking about an ingredient in a different way. The depth and bitterness of the radicchio balances well with the richness of the ham and beans. I think more about flavors and less about an ingredient's traditional use. Serve this hearty main course with a hunk of garlic bread and a glass of Côtes du Rhône. Any leftover stew works well as a taco or burrito filling the next day. ■ **SERVES 6 TO 8**

¼ cup extra-virgin olive oil, plus more for brushing the radicchio and finishing

2 celery stalks, cut into 1-inch chunks

1 large carrot, cut into 1-inch chunks

1 medium onion, chopped (about 1 cup)

4 garlic cloves, chopped

2 tablespoons smoked paprika

1 tablespoon herbes de Provence

2 tablespoons tomato paste

3 15-ounce cans black beans, rinsed and drained

1 cup dry white wine

1 large or 2 small meaty ham hocks (about 1½ pounds total)

1 dried bay leaf

2 small heads radicchio, cut into eighths, cored, trimmed but still attached at the core

Kosher salt

1 cup crème fraîche

¼ cup chopped fresh Italian parsley

1 Preheat the oven to 350°F. In a large Dutch oven, heat the oil over medium heat. Add the celery, carrot, and onion. Cook until the onion is translucent, about 6 minutes. Add the garlic, paprika, and herbes de Provence and cook until fragrant, about 1 minute. Make a space in the pan and add the tomato paste there, allowing it to toast for 1 minute before stirring it into the vegetables. Stir in the beans, raise the heat to high, and add the white wine. Boil until the wine is almost evaporated, about 3 minutes. Just a film of syrupy wine should be left in the pan.

2 Add 6 cups water and tuck the ham hocks and bay leaf into the liquid. Bring to a simmer, cover, and bake for 1 hour. Raise the heat to 400°F., uncover, stir in up to 1 cup more water if the stew seems dry, and bake until the stew is crusty on top and the ham hocks are very tender, 30 to 40 minutes more. Remove the ham hocks and let cool slightly.

3 Meanwhile, heat a grill pan over medium-high heat. Brush the radicchio with oil and grill until charred and slightly wilted on both sides, about 5 minutes total. Remove to a plate and season with salt.

4 In a medium bowl, lightly whip the crème fraîche.

5 When the ham hocks are cool enough to handle, remove any meat, finely chop, and add back to the stew.

6 To serve, warm the stew and stir in the parsley. Discard the bay leaf. Put the stew in a shallow serving bowl. Top with the grilled radicchio and a drizzle of olive oil and serve the whipped crème fraîche on the side.

7 BEANS
CANNELLINI, DRIED

Cannellini beans are an Italian staple. They are the shape and size of a kidney bean but are creamy white in color. Once cooked, they have a fluffy texture inside and a slightly nutty, earthy flavor.

To cook cannellini beans, soak them in water in the refrigerator overnight. Drain, rinse, and add more cold water to cover (I like to throw in a bay leaf, too). Bring to a simmer and cook until tender, about an hour, depending on the age of your beans. Let them cool in the cooking liquid as it helps maintain their creamy texture.

Tips

- Canned cannellinis can be substituted in recipes calling for cooked beans. Two cans equals about 3 cups.

- One cup of dried beans will yield 2½ to 3 cups cooked, which is what I use for these recipes.

SPICED BEAN DIP

This dip is fantastic with crudité, pita, or crackers or spread on a toasted baguette with roasted peppers or tomatoes on top. I also like it as a sandwich spread, topped with roasted vegetables or crunchy raw shredded vegetables and sprouts. The fragrance of the garlic and spices makes this a smart starter for a cocktail party. ■ SERVES 6 TO 8

½ cup extra-virgin olive oil

6 garlic cloves, crushed

½ teaspoon ground cumin

½ teaspoon smoked paprika

¼ teaspoon ground cinnamon

¼ teaspoon ground fennel seed

¼ teaspoon crushed red pepper flakes

⅛ teaspoon ground cardamom

3 cups cooked and drained cannellini beans

Juice of 2 lemons (about 6 tablespoons)

Kosher salt

2 tablespoons pine nuts, toasted

Pita chips, crackers, or crudité, for dipping

1 In a small saucepan, heat the oil and garlic over low heat. Let the garlic gently bubble in the oil until it has softened but hasn't taken on any color, about 5 minutes. Stir in the cumin, paprika, cinnamon, fennel, pepper flakes, and cardamom and let toast until fragrant, about 1 minute. Remove from the heat and let cool 10 minutes.

2 Add the beans and lemon juice to a food processor. Add the cooked garlic cloves and all but 1 tablespoon of the spiced oil. Puree to make a smooth dip, season with salt, and puree again. Spoon the dip into a wide bowl and sprinkle with the pine nuts. Drizzle the remaining 1 tablespoon of spiced oil over the dip and serve.

LAMB AND BEAN SALAD
WITH APRICOTS AND OLIVES

The beans, which get plated under the sliced lamb, act as a starch soaking up the lamb jus. As a result, the salad of beans, apricots, and olives gets an added savory kick from the cooked marinade, jus, and spices from the meat. This marinade is also great for lamb and vegetable kebabs on the grill, and it works well with chicken, too. ■ SERVES 4

LAMB

1 small onion, cut in chunks

6 garlic cloves, crushed

1 cup fresh cilantro leaves

1 cup fresh Italian parsley leaves

1 tablespoon ground cumin

2 teaspoons smoked paprika

½ teaspoon ground ginger

¼ teaspoon cayenne

Juice of 2 lemons (about 6 tablespoons)

½ cup extra-virgin olive oil, plus more for brushing the grill

1¼ pounds boneless leg of lamb, trimmed of fat and sinew

Kosher salt and freshly ground black pepper

BEAN SALAD

4 tablespoons extra-virgin olive oil, plus more for drizzling

1 bunch scallions, white and green parts, chopped (about 1 cup)

3 garlic cloves, sliced

1 teaspoon ground cumin

1 teaspoon smoked paprika

3 cups cooked cannellini beans, drained

½ cup sliced dried apricots

½ cup pitted and halved large green olives, such as Cerignola

Juice of 2 lemons (about 6 tablespoons)

2 teaspoons honey

Kosher salt and freshly ground black pepper

¼ cup chopped fresh cilantro

¼ chopped fresh Italian parsley

4 cups baby arugula, washed and dried

❙ To make the lamb: In a food processor, combine the onion, garlic, cilantro, parsley, cumin, paprika, ginger, cayenne, and lemon juice. Process to make a chunky paste. With the motor running, add the oil and process until smooth. Pour into a baking dish large enough to also fit the lamb.

2 Lay the lamb on a cutting board and use a meat mallet to pound to an even thickness of about 2 inches. Season with salt and pepper and add to the marinade, turning to coat. Cover with plastic wrap and marinate overnight in the refrigerator.

3 When you are ready to cook the lamb, remove it from the refrigerator and pat dry. Let the lamb sit at room temperature while you heat the grill to medium high. When the grill is ready, brush with oil. Grill the lamb, turning once, until the lamb reaches an internal temperature of 125°F. for medium rare, about 5 minutes per side. Let rest while you make the bean salad.

4 To make the bean salad: In a large skillet over medium heat, add 3 tablespoons of the oil. When the oil is hot, add the scallions and garlic and cook until wilted, about 3 minutes. Add the cumin and paprika and cook until fragrant, about 1 minute. Stir in the beans, apricots, olives, ¼ cup of the lemon juice, and the honey. Add ¾ cup water, bring to a simmer, and season with salt and pepper. Simmer just to bring the flavors together and soften the apricots, about 5 minutes. Stir in the cilantro and parsley and drizzle with a little more oil.

5 When you're ready to serve, thinly slice the lamb against the grain. In a medium bowl, toss the arugula with the remaining 1 tablespoon oil and remaining lemon juice. Season with salt and pepper. Spoon the beans onto serving plates, then top with the thinly sliced lamb. Mound the arugula on top and serve.

LAMB AND BEAN SALAD
WITH APRICOTS AND OLIVES

VEAL AND BEAN CASSEROLE

SPICED BEAN DIP

VEAL AND BEAN CASSEROLE

Cannellini beans are an excellent choice for casseroles, because they soak up the cooking juices and become extra creamy in texture. ■ SERVES 4 TO 6

½ ounce dried porcini mushrooms

1 cup boiling water

¼ cup plus 1 tablespoon extra-virgin olive oil

2 pounds veal shoulder, cut into 1-inch cubes

Kosher salt and freshly ground black pepper

1 medium onion, chopped (about 1 cup)

1 large carrot, cut in 1-inch chunks

2 celery stalks, cut in 1-inch chunks

2 garlic cloves, sliced

2 tablespoons chopped fresh sage

¼ cup tomato paste

1 cup white wine

2 dried bay leaves

Zest of 1 small orange, removed with a vegetable peeler in large strips and the orange itself juiced

3 cups cooked cannellini beans, drained

½ cup fine dry bread crumbs

¼ cup chopped fresh Italian parsley

1 Preheat the oven to 350°F. Place the porcini in a small heat-proof bowl and pour in the boiling water; soak for 15 minutes. Remove the porcini, squeeze dry, and finely chop. Strain and reserve the soaking liquid.

2 In a large Dutch oven, heat ¼ cup of the oil over medium-high heat. Pat the veal dry and season with salt and pepper. Brown the veal in 2 batches until well browned all over, about 5 minutes per batch, then remove to a plate. Add the onion, carrot, and celery and cook until lightly caramelized, about 6 minutes. Add the garlic and sage and cook until fragrant, about 1 minute. Make a space in the pan and add the tomato paste, then stir in that spot until the paste darkens a shade or two, 1 to 2 minutes. Stir the paste into the vegetables. Add the wine, bay leaves, and orange zest and juice and cook until the liquid is reduced by half. Add the veal, 3 cups water, and the porcini liquid. Season with salt and pepper. Bring to a simmer, cover, and bake until the veal is just tender, about 1 hour.

3 Stir in the cannellini beans and enough water to keep the mixture saucy, about 1 cup. Cover and cook until the veal is very tender, about 30 minutes more. Remove the bay leave.

4 In a small bowl, stir together the bread crumbs, 1 tablespoon oil, and the parsley. Sprinkle the mixture over the casserole and bake, uncovered, until the crumbs are golden brown, about 10 minutes at 425°F. Serve hot.

BEANS
LIMA, DRIED

Lima beans originated in Peru almost eight thousand years ago. They are eaten in many parts of the world and are a popular staple in the American South, where they are often called butter beans because of their creamy texture and color.

　　To cook limas, soak them overnight in plenty of cold water. Then drain and add fresh water so it covers the beans. Simmer until tender, 35 to 40 minutes, checking frequently toward the end, as limas quickly get mushy. It is important to get the cooking and seasoning of this bean correct, otherwise you will be continuing the maligned legacy that limas have. That bad reputation among Americans comes from decades of poor cooking execution! Baby limas are preferable over the large ones as they hold their shape better and don't dwarf other ingredients, but either will work.

Tips

- A half pound of dried limas yields 2 cups cooked, which is what is needed for these recipes.

- Limas are one of the only beans I don't like canned, because of the texture. I prefer dried.

LIMA, CORN, AND
FRESH HERB SALAD

SUCCOTASH

LIMA BEAN HASH WITH
POACHED EGGS

LIMA, CORN, AND FRESH HERB SALAD

The earthy flavor of lima beans balances the sweet corn and tomatoes, and the beans soak up the dressing well. This chunky salad can work as a side dish to accompany pork, chicken, or fish. To make it a lovely, light main-course salad, add about a pound of cooked and chopped shrimp or lobster. Use any combination of young fresh herbs, and if the leaves are small enough add them whole, or tear larger ones into rough pieces. ■ **SERVES 4**

4 tablespoons extra-virgin olive oil

1½ cups fresh corn kernels (from about 3 ears of corn)

2 cups cooked lima beans, cooled

1 cup halved cherry tomatoes

Juice of 2 limes (about 2 tablespoons)

1 teaspoon honey

Kosher salt

2 cups mixed fresh herbs, such as any combination of basil, cilantro, chives, mint, and Italian parsley

1 In a medium skillet, heat 1 tablespoon of the oil over medium-high heat. When the oil is hot, add the corn. Cook and toss until the corn is just tender, 2 to 3 minutes. Scrape into a serving bowl.

2 To the bowl, add the lima beans, tomatoes, lime juice, honey, and remaining 3 tablespoons oil. Season with salt and toss. Let the salad sit 15 minutes to let the flavors develop.

3 When ready to serve, add the mixed herbs, toss gently, and serve.

LIMA BEAN HASH WITH POACHED EGGS

For crispy-on-the-outside, creamy-on-the-inside hash, it's important to let it sit in the pan and develop a nice crust before flipping. If you stir too much, your hash will turn to mush. Lima beans are starchy and a particularly good choice in hash to help hold it together and form a crust. ■ SERVES 4

2 tablespoons (¼ stick) unsalted butter

1 tablespoon extra-virgin olive oil

2 ounces pancetta, diced

1 small onion, chopped (about 1 cup)

1 small red bell pepper, cored, seeded, and chopped

1 large russet potato, peeled and diced small

1 jalapeño, finely chopped (leave in the seeds if you want some heat)

Kosher salt

2 cups cooked lima beans

1 bunch scallions, white and green parts, chopped (about 1 cup)

1 tablespoon chopped fresh thyme leaves

2 tablespoons chopped fresh Italian parsley

1 teaspoon white wine or cider vinegar

4 large eggs

1 Bring 2 inches of water to a simmer in a large nonstick skillet. In another large skillet, over medium heat, add 1 tablespoon butter, the oil, and pancetta. Cook and stir until the pancetta begins to render its fat but is not yet crisp, about 3 minutes.

2 Add the onion, bell pepper, potato, and jalapeño. Cook, stirring and tossing occasionally, until the vegetables are softened and the potatoes are browned and tender, about 10 minutes. Season with salt.

3 Raise the heat to medium-high and add the beans, scallions, and thyme. Let sit in the skillet, without stirring, until the hash develops a crust on the bottom, about 2 minutes. Flip and stir and let sit until a crust develops again, 2 to 3 minutes more. Stir in the parsley and keep warm. Then poach the eggs. Stir the vinegar into the simmering water. Carefully crack the eggs, 1 at a time, into a ramekin or small bowl, and slide into the simmering water without breaking the yolks. Simmer the eggs until done to your liking, about 4 minutes for fully set whites with a still runny yolk.

4 Divide the hash onto 4 plates. Remove the eggs from the water with a slotted spoon, blot briefly on a kitchen towel to dry, and serve an egg atop each portion.

SUCCOTASH

Succotash is an iconic American dish and lima beans are the key ingredient. Their somewhat bland flavor and starchy texture soak up all of the cooking juices, leaving them richly flavored. This recipe contains the classic components, but once you have it down, you can riff on it with other ingredients, by adding bacon or ham, chopped tomato, fresh jalapeño, and fresh herbs of your choice. Succotash is a great side to crispy fried chicken or baked ham.

■ **SERVES 4 TO 6**

2 tablespoons (¼ stick) unsalted butter

I small red bell pepper, cored, seeded, and diced

I bunch scallions, white and green parts, chopped (about I cup)

I tablespoon chopped fresh thyme

2 cups cooked lima beans

2 cups fresh corn kernels (from about 4 ears of corn)

½ cup chicken stock

½ cup heavy cream

¼ cup chopped fresh Italian parsley

Juice of ½ lemon

1 In a large skillet over medium heat, add the butter. When the butter is melted, add the bell pepper and scallions and cook, stirring occasionally until wilted, about 4 minutes. Add the thyme and cook until fragrant, about 1 minute.

2 Add the lima beans and corn and toss to combine. Pour in the stock and cream and bring to a rapid simmer. Cook until the sauce has thickened and coats the vegetables, about 3 minutes. Stir in the parsley and lemon juice and serve.

9 BREAD CRUMBS

Bread crumbs, found in various cuisines throughout history, provide an efficient use for dry day-old bread. Truly the unsung hero of the pantry, this workhorse has so many uses— some obvious and some hidden, as you will see in the recipes that follow. Bread crumbs can be made from any type of bread as long as it is dried out, and once in crumb form, seasoning can be added as well. I prefer unseasoned freshly made bread crumbs from two-day-old French bread with the crust. Just rough-cut and process in a food processor until the crumbs have a pebbled sandlike consistency. If starting with fresh bread, you can lightly toast on a sheet tray in the oven to speed up the dehydrating process or let air dry.

If you are not making fresh bread crumbs, try to buy from a local bakery or the bakery area in your grocery store. Avoid preseasoned bread crumbs as they are generally high in artificial flavors and sodium.

Tips

- Use fresh bread crumbs within I week or freeze in an airtight container.

- A sprinkle of bread crumbs is a great last-minute addition to thicken a sauce or stew.

MAGNIFICENT MEATBALLS

Here bread crumbs and pureed onions magically act to bind the proteins and keep the meat moist and almost creamy. Although undetectable in the end result, these tricks will serve you well. ■ **MAKES ABOUT 2 DOZEN MEDIUM MEATBALLS, DEPENDING ON WHICH FAMILY RAISED YOU!**

1 large onion, cut into chunks

3 garlic cloves

1 pound ground pork

1 pound ground veal

2 large eggs

1/2 cup freshly grated Parmigiano-Reggiano, plus more for serving

1/2 cup freshly grated Pecorino Romano

1 1/2 cups unseasoned fresh bread crumbs

1/4 cup chopped fresh Italian parsley

Pinch of crushed red pepper flakes

Kosher salt and freshly ground black pepper

Canola and olive oil, for frying

1 In a food processor, combine the onion, garlic, and 1 cup water. Puree until very smooth. In a large mixing bowl, combine the pork, veal, eggs, Parmigiano-Reggiano, Pecorino Romano, bread crumbs, parsley, pepper flakes, and salt and pepper. Add the onion puree and, with your hands, mix until *just* combined. Form 1 small meatball and fry, just to taste for seasoning, and adjust if necessary.

2 Wet your hands and form the meat mixture into 24 meatballs. Don't overwork the mixture—the meatballs should be light and soft, not spongy and tough. Put the meatballs on a rimmed sheet pan and refrigerate 30 minutes to firm them up.

3 Preheat the oven to 350°F. When ready to fry, in a large skillet over medium heat, heat enough canola and olive oil (equal amounts of each) to come one third of the way up the sides of the meatballs. Fry the meatballs, in batches, until browned all over, about 6 minutes per batch. Drain and place on a rimmed sheet pan. When all the meatballs are browned, place in the oven and bake until cooked through, about 15 minutes. (The browned meatballs can also be finished by simmering in marinara or another tomato sauce for 30 minutes.) Serve with heaps of finely shredded Parmigiano-Reggiano.

MAGNIFICENT
MEATBALLS

ROASTED CARROTS WITH
PROVENÇAL BREAD CRUMB CRUST

FAMILY CHICKEN
FINGERS

FAMILY CHICKEN FINGERS

It is worth every effort to make fresh chicken fingers rather than defaulting to the prebreaded frozen kind. Elevate this crowd pleaser by using superb butter, quality chicken, and bread crumbs seasoned with fresh Parmigiano-Reggiano. Usually, there are none left over, but just in case, cut-up chicken fingers make for a great sandwich the next day drizzled with creamy blue cheese dressing and topped with shredded romaine lettuce. Once you make these a few times, it will be difficult for you and your children to consider consuming the store-bought frozen variety. ■ **SERVES 4 TO 6 CHILDREN**

1½ pounds boneless, skinless chicken breast, sliced into 3 × ½-inch strips

Kosher salt and freshly ground black pepper

2 large eggs

2 tablespoons extra-virgin olive oil, plus more for frying

1 cup dry bread crumbs

1 cup freshly grated Parmigiano-Reggiano

1 tablespoon chopped fresh thyme

2 tablespoons (¼ stick) unsalted butter

Creamy blue cheese dressing or ketchup, for dipping

1 Preheat the oven to 250°F. Season the chicken strips with salt and pepper. In a large, shallow pan, beat the eggs with the oil. In another shallow pan, combine the bread crumbs, cheese, and thyme.

2 In 2 or 3 batches, dredge the chicken in the eggs, then in the bread crumbs. For extra-crispy chicken fingers, dredge one more time in the eggs and bread crumbs. Then put the chicken on a parchment-lined rimmed sheet pan while you dredge the remaining batches.

3 In a large, preferably nonstick skillet, heat about ½ inch oil over medium heat. Melt the butter in the oil. Once the oil is hot enough that a touch of the bread crumb mixture bubbles when sprinkled on top, add a batch of chicken fingers. Fry until crispy and golden brown on both sides and cooked through, about 3 minutes per side.

4 Drain on a paper-towel-lined rimmed sheet pan. Keep the chicken fingers warm in the preheated oven while you fry the remaining batches. Serve immediately, with creamy blue cheese dressing or ketchup on the side.

ROASTED CARROTS
WITH PROVENÇAL BREAD CRUMB CRUST

Carrots are a workhorse vegetable, but the use here of the bread crumb crust gives the carrot a luxurious makeover and allows it to take center stage. You can substitute tomatoes for carrots altogether in this recipe, too. Simply slice the tomatoes, top with the bread crumb mixture, and bake until juices are bubbling and the crumbs are crisp and browned.

■ **SERVES 6 OR MORE AS A SIDE**

Kosher salt

2 pounds baby carrots with tops, trimmed to leave a small tip of green at the top

¼ cup extra-virgin olive oil, plus more for drizzling

Freshly ground black pepper

2 cups unseasoned fresh bread crumbs

2 small shallots, finely chopped

½ cup chopped fresh basil

½ cup chopped fresh Italian parsley

½ cup chopped scallions, white and green parts

2 garlic cloves, finely chopped

¼ cup freshly grated Parmigiano-Reggiano

1 Preheat the oven to 375°F. Bring a large pot of salted water to a boil. Blanch the carrots until just tender but still al dente, about 4 minutes. Drain and cool in an ice bath. Pat dry on paper towels. Arrange in a single layer in a glass or ceramic baking dish and drizzle with a little oil. Season with salt and pepper.

2 In a large bowl, combine the bread crumbs, shallots, basil, parsley, scallions, and garlic. Season with salt and pepper. Drizzle with the oil and toss well with a fork to combine.

3 Sprinkle the crumb mixture over the carrots so the carrots are almost completely obscured by the crumbs. Sprinkle with the cheese and drizzle with a bit more oil. Roast until the carrots are browned and the crumbs are crisp and golden, 20 to 25 minutes. Serve family style while still hot.

10 CHICKPEAS

Chickpeas, also known in America as ceci beans and garbanzo beans, are part of the pea family and grow inside pods that hang from a short bushy plant. One of the oldest beans known to man, chickpeas are extremely hearty and high in protein.

Dried chickpeas are one of the trickiest dried beans to cook, so for ease, I turn to canned chickpeas. These beans have a nutty quality and a firm skin that yields to a creamy interior. Chickpeas hold their shape in a variety of preparations but also puree well without any additional cooking, such as in hummus. Quite mild, chickpeas work well with many types of ingredients and can be used in a number of cuisines.

Tips

■ When using canned chickpeas, be sure to rinse them thoroughly.

■ If using dried chickpeas, soak them overnight and then the next day simmer until tender (1 to 2 hours or refer to packaging for cook time).

FRIED CHICKPEA SALAD

Make sure to dry the chickpeas very well, which will allow them to get crisp and golden on the outside while remaining creamy inside. This salad is best served when the chickpeas are slightly warm or at room temperature.

■ SERVES 4

⅓ cup Greek yogurt

3 tablespoons fresh lemon juice

5 tablespoons extra-virgin olive oil

Kosher salt and freshly ground black pepper

1 15-ounce can chickpeas, rinsed, drained, and dried very well

1 bunch scallions, white and green parts, coarsely chopped (about 1 cup)

3 garlic cloves, sliced

1 teaspoon ground cumin

3 cups baby arugula, washed and dried

3 cups baby kale, washed and dried

1½ cups halved cherry tomatoes

½ cup coarsely chopped fresh cilantro

½ cup coarsely chopped fresh mint

¼ cup finely crumbled feta cheese

2 tablespoons pine nuts, toasted

1 In a small bowl, stir together the yogurt, lemon juice, and 1 tablespoon of the oil. Season with salt and pepper. Set aside.

2 In a large skillet over high heat, add 3 tablespoons of the oil. When the oil is hot, add the chickpeas. Cook, tossing occasionally, until they're golden and crisp on the exterior, 6 to 7 minutes.

3 Reduce the heat to medium high and add the scallions, garlic, and cumin. Cook and stir until the scallions just begin to wilt, about 2 minutes. Transfer to a large serving bowl and let cool slightly, about 15 minutes.

4 Add the arugula, kale, tomatoes, cilantro, mint, cheese, and pine nuts to the bowl with the chickpeas. Pour over the yogurt dressing, season with salt and pepper, and drizzle with the remaining 1 tablespoon oil. Toss well and serve.

CHICKPEA TARTARE

The chickpeas lend a healthy dose of protein to this vegetable tartare. The soft texture of the chickpeas and the crunch of the vegetables make for an interesting and balanced bite. To turn this salad into a light main course, add some cooked shrimp or chicken. Any leftover salad keeps well in the refrigerator for a day or two. And if you cannot find ricotta salata, feta makes for a nice alternative. ■ **SERVES 4 TO 6**

¼ cup finely chopped red onion

2 15-ounce cans chickpeas, rinsed, drained, and dried well

2 plum tomatoes, cored, seeded, and diced (about 1 cup)

½ cup chopped Kalamata olives

¼ cup chopped fresh Italian parsley

1 garlic clove, finely chopped

¼ cup extra-virgin olive oil

2 tablespoons white wine vinegar

Kosher salt and freshly ground black pepper

½ cup shaved ricotta salata

¼ teaspoon dried oregano

Juice of ½ lemon (about 1½ tablespoons)

1 Put the onion in a strainer and rinse with cold water to remove some of the bite. Pat dry with paper towels.

2 In a serving bowl, combine the onion, chickpeas, tomatoes, olives, parsley, and garlic. Drizzle with the oil and vinegar, season with salt and pepper, and toss well.

3 Top with a sprinkle of the ricotta salata, dried oregano, and lemon juice and serve.

CHICKPEA TARTARE

FRIED CHICKPEA SALAD

HANGER STEAK AND CHICKPEA SALAD WITH ARUGULA PESTO

HANGER STEAK AND CHICKPEA SALAD WITH ARUGULA PESTO

The key to this recipe is using just enough of the arugula pesto to coat the chickpea salad. It is imperative not to use too much, because the arugula pesto is potent and needs to be enjoyed in balanced quantities. You can use the little bit of leftover pesto in any way you would use regular basil pesto—for pasta, pizza, as a sandwich spread, or as a last-minute stir-in for a soup or stew. To stretch this salad to serve six, add another can of chickpeas and use all the pesto and an extra lemon. ■ **SERVES 4**

STEAK AND SALAD

I teaspoon freshly ground black pepper

I teaspoon celery salt

I teaspoon sugar

¼ teaspoon cayenne

I hanger steak (about I¾ pounds)

2 tablespoons extra-virgin olive oil

I 15-ounce can chickpeas, rinsed and drained

I½ cups halved cherry tomatoes

I large shallot, very thinly sliced

2 tablespoons pine nuts, toasted

Juice of I lemon (about 3 tablespoons)

ARUGULA PESTO

3 cups packed baby arugula, washed and dried

I cup packed fresh Italian parsley leaves

I garlic clove

3 tablespoons pine nuts, toasted

¼ cup extra-virgin olive oil

¼ cup freshly grated Parmigiano-Reggiano

Kosher salt and freshly ground black pepper

1 To make the steak: In a small bowl, combine the pepper, celery salt, sugar, and cayenne. Rub the mixture all over the steak and then drizzle with the oil and rub again to coat the steak. Wrap in plastic and let marinate in the refrigerator for at least 8 hours or overnight.

2 To make the pesto: In a food processor, combine the arugula, parsley, garlic, and pine nuts. Pulse to make a chunky paste. With the machine running, drizzle in the oil to make an almost smooth sauce. Scrape into a medium bowl, stir in the cheese, and season with salt and pepper. Cover and set aside while you grill the steak.

3 Remove the steak from the refrigerator 30 minutes before you're ready to cook to come to room temperature. Preheat a grill or grill pan to medium high. Grill, turning once, until the internal temperature reads 125°F. for medium rare, about 12 minutes. Let rest on a cutting board 10 minutes before slicing.

4 In a large bowl, combine the chickpeas, tomatoes, shallot, and pine nuts. Add about half the pesto and all the lemon juice and toss to coat, adding a little more pesto if necessary to lightly coat the salad.

5 To slice the hanger steak, thinly slice against the grain on both long sides of the steak, stopping at the muscle that runs down the center of the steak. Put the chickpea salad on a platter and top with the sliced steak and a few dollops of pesto.

11 CHOCOLATE
SEMISWEET

Semisweet chocolate, also referred to as dark chocolate, is made by combining cocoa, cocoa butter, and sugar. All types of chocolates (bittersweet, semisweet, milk) have varying proportions of ingredients, but for semisweet the rule of thumb is half the amount of sugar as cocoa. Chocolate contains different percentages of cocoa, with the lower percentages indicating higher milk content and the higher percentages indicating higher cocoa content. Semisweet chocolate is in the range of 60% to 70%.

Chocolate is like a drug to me. I prefer around 70% cocoa content, and I never tire of the flavor. I try to enjoy at least one portion of chocolate every afternoon with a double espresso. In my chocolate endeavors, I have also come to appreciate the different worldwide origins of cocoa beans and how they translate into the end flavor. I strongly suggest taking the time to taste test a few different chocolates that come from various parts of the world.

Tips

- For long-term storage, wrap chocolate well in plastic wrap and keep in the freezer.

- Use a serrated knife to chop chocolate.

- When you need to melt chocolate, always use a double boiler. The low heat prevents chocolate from seizing while melting, and keeps it silky smooth.

- Chocolate can develop a dusty gray coating on the outside called bloom. It's still safe to use, and the grayness will disappear once melted.

CHOCOLATE MUFFINS

Do not confuse these muffins, although chocolate, with cupcakes, as they are not overly sweet. This recipe strikes the perfect balance so they can be eaten for breakfast or as a not-terribly-guilty snack with a hot cup of coffee. I like to serve these as part of a weekend brunch or on their own when friends might be stopping by for a visit. You can also make these in a mini size (be sure to cut the baking time) so the portion is more suitable for a children's snack. ■ **MAKES A DOZEN MUFFINS**

6 ounces semisweet chocolate, chopped

¼ pound (1 stick) unsalted butter, cut into chunks

2 cups all-purpose flour

2 teaspoons baking powder

½ teaspoon baking soda

¼ teaspoon fine salt

2 large eggs

¾ cup (packed) dark brown sugar

⅔ cup buttermilk

1 teaspoon pure vanilla extract

1 cup chocolate chunks or chips

1 Preheat the oven to 350°F. Line 12 muffin cups with paper liners. Melt the semisweet chocolate and the butter together in a double boiler and stir until smooth. Let cool slightly.

2 Sift together the flour, baking powder, baking soda, and salt. Set aside.

3 In a large bowl, whisk together the eggs and sugar until smooth and then whisk in the buttermilk and vanilla. Drizzle in the melted chocolate mixture, whisking constantly until smooth. Add the sifted flour mixture and stir with a wooden spoon until just combined; don't overmix. Stir in the chocolate chunks or chips.

4 Divide the batter among the muffin cups. Bake on the middle rack until a tester inserted in the center of a muffin comes out clean, about 18 minutes. Cool on a wire cooling rack before serving.

CHOCOLATE MUFFINS

DARK CHOCOLATE PUDDING

CHOCOLATE-DIPPED
CANDIED ORANGES

CHOCOLATE-DIPPED CANDIED ORANGES

Chocolate and orange is an irresistible age-old flavor combination. Valencia oranges have floral notes and the correct balance of acid to enhance and hold up to the candying process and ultimately to the chocolate. The syrup left over from candying the oranges is a deliciously orangey, bittersweet by-product, so don't throw it away! It can be used to sweeten iced tea or even bourbon cocktails. You can use this same dipping method for store-bought dried fruit, such as apricots, pears, figs, or candied ginger slices.

■ **MAKES ABOUT 40 PIECES**

2 Valencia oranges

3$\frac{1}{2}$ cups sugar

12 ounces semisweet chocolate

1 Cut the oranges lengthwise. Place on a board cut side down and slice into $\frac{1}{4}$-inch half-moons, discarding the ends and any seeds.

2 In a 10-inch straight-sided sauté pan, bring 3 cups water and the sugar to a boil over medium heat. Add the orange slices. Simmer over medium-low heat, turning the slices occasionally, until the orange slices are translucent and tender, about 45 minutes. Remove from the syrup with a fork or tongs and drain on a wire rack set over a rimmed sheet pan. Let dry at room temperature 24 hours to 48 hours, until almost dry, though they will still be a little sticky.

3 When the slices are dry, melt the chocolate in a double boiler. Dip one end of each candied orange slice in the chocolate, allowing the excess to drip back into the pan. Place the dipped orange slices on parchment-lined sheet pans and let the chocolate harden completely, about 2 hours. You can put them in the fridge to expedite this process, about 30 minutes.

DARK CHOCOLATE PUDDING

This is a dense chocolate pudding as opposed to a ready-made "loose" one you might buy at the grocery store. Because of the rich quality, it does well when cut with a bit of whipped cream for serving. If you don't like a skin on the top of your pudding, cover the surface with plastic wrap or rounds of parchment while still warm. This pudding can be made one or two days ahead, but keep it covered so it doesn't pick up other flavors from the refrigerator. ■ **SERVES 4**

6 ounces semisweet chocolate, chopped

¾ cup heavy cream

½ cup whole milk

4 large egg yolks

⅓ cup sugar

1 teaspoon pure vanilla extract

Pinch of fine salt

Classic Whipped Cream (page 233), for serving (optional)

1 Melt the chocolate in a double boiler over low heat. In a medium saucepan, bring the cream and milk to a bare simmer. In a large bowl, whisk together the egg yolks, sugar, vanilla, and salt.

2 Slowly pour the milk mixture into the egg mixture to temper it, whisking all the while. Return the mixture to the saucepan and cook over low heat until the mixture coats the back of a spoon, about 4 minutes. Pour in the melted chocolate and whisk until smooth.

3 Pour into glasses or custard cups. Refrigerate until chilled and set, about 3 hours. Serve with whipped cream, if desired.

12 COCOA POWDER

Theobroma cacao (roughly translated as "the food of gods") grows within twenty degrees of the equator, and although native to South America, it is now grown mostly in West Africa. Large pods are harvested from the tree and cracked open, and the seeds are left to dry. From there, the seeds can be made into cocoa nibs, cocoa butter, and cocoa powder.

There are two kinds of cocoa powder—natural and Dutch process. Natural cocoa, which is what you most often see in your grocery store (think Hershey's), is lighter in color and has a slight edge of acidity to it. Dutch-process cocoa is darker in color and more neutral. If a baking recipe calls for cocoa powder and you don't know which to use, use natural cocoa if the recipe contains baking soda, and use Dutch process if the recipe contains baking powder. For these recipes, I used natural.

Tips

- It is worthwhile to pay a bit more for this ingredient. It will ensure a good cacao plant lineage and a more robust chocolate flavor in your dish.

- Cocoa powder will keep up to a year, tightly sealed, in your pantry. Don't keep it in the refrigerator, as moisture will make it clump and harden.

CHOCOLATE SMOOTHIE

Cocoa powder is not too sweet, so the honey makes up for that and marries well with the Greek yogurt. Be sure to use *whole* milk and *whole* yogurt as the fat content will keep the drink creamy. Cocoa powder is the quickest way to add a hit of chocolate without adding sugar. ■ **SERVES 4**

2 cups cold whole milk

½ cup honey

½ cup whole milk Greek yogurt

⅓ cup natural cocoa powder

2 cups ice cubes

Chill 4 glasses in the freezer for 30 minutes before you want to serve the smoothie. Put the milk, honey, yogurt, cocoa, and ice cubes in a blender and blend on high until smooth and creamy. Pour into the chilled glasses and serve right away.

CHOCOLATE SORBET

Cocoa powder lends a bittersweet flavor to this sorbet. Feel free to add one or two tablespoons of your favorite liqueur for a slightly more sophisticated flavor. ■ SERVES 4

1 cup sugar

½ cup natural cocoa powder

1 teaspoon instant espresso

Pinch of kosher salt

1 Bring 2 cups water to a simmer in a medium saucepan. Whisk in the sugar, cocoa, espresso, and salt until smooth. Bring to a simmer over medium heat, cook just until the sugar dissolves, and then remove from the heat. Carefully blend, with a hand blender or in a countertop blender, until completely smooth.

2 Chill in the refrigerator until very cold, at least 2 hours, and then freeze in an ice-cream maker according to the manufacturer's instructions. The sorbet will be softly set when you remove it from the machine. Cover and freeze until firm, about 4 hours or overnight.

CHOCOLATE
SMOOTHIE

CHOCOLATE
SORBET

CHOCOLATE
MERINGUES

CHOCOLATE MERINGUES

Plain meringues are pure sweetness. Adding cocoa powder gives them the slightest hint of bitterness that I find more appealing. It can be tricky to gauge the "doneness" of meringues. Start checking after two hours, but if you are making them on a very wet or humid day, it may take an additional half hour or more for them to dry out. Meringues are great when served with or after dessert. ▪ **MAKES ABOUT 2½ DOZEN MERINGUES**

3 tablespoons natural cocoa powder

3 large egg whites, at room temperature

¼ teaspoon cream of tartar

½ cup sugar

1 Preheat the oven to 250°F. Sift the cocoa onto a piece of parchment paper. Line a rimmed sheet pan with parchment or a silicone baking mat.

2 Put the egg whites and cream of tartar in the bowl of an electric mixer and beat on medium speed until foamy. Increase the speed to high and pour in the sugar in a steady stream. Beat until the egg whites form firm peaks. Reduce the speed to low, pour in the sifted cocoa, and whisk until just combined. Increase the speed to high once more and mix just until the cocoa is incorporated completely.

3 Put the meringue in a pastry bag fitted with a large star tip. Pipe in rosettes, the width of a quarter, onto the lined pan. Bake on the middle rack of the oven, turning the pan occasionally, until the meringues are dry and crisp throughout, 2 to 2½ hours.

COCONUT MILK

13

Coconut palms grow in warm, humid climates such as the southern parts of Florida, Hawaii, and Madagascar. Technically known as a drupe and not a nut, the coconut is the fruit of the palm tree and can take up to a year to ripen. Other than whole, you can purchase coconut in three main forms: coconut water, dried coconut, and coconut milk.

Coconut water, a natural source of electrolytes, is simply the water inside a fresh coconut. Dried coconut is the shaved, dried flesh of the coconut and is available sweetened or unsweetened. And coconut milk is extracted from pressing the white flesh of the coconut and it usually comes canned. Mainly used for sauces, soups, and curries, coconut milk adds a sweet and subtle richness to dishes.

Tips

- Use light coconut milk as a healthier option if you're concerned about fat.

- Coconut milk should always be stirred or shaken before using.

- When making rice, you can substitute I cup of coconut milk for I cup of water to infuse a mild coconut flavor into the grains.

CURRIED COCONUT SOUP
WITH LEMONGRASS AND SPRING GARLIC

This light soup is full of flavor as is but can also be made heartier with a last-minute addition of some crabmeat or coarsely chopped shrimp. I prefer to eat this in the cooler months of spring, but in the summer, it can also be served chilled. ■ SERVES 4

2 tablespoons extra-virgin olive oil

½ cup thinly sliced onion

½ cup thinly sliced spring garlic, scallions, or spring onions (white and light green parts)

¼ cup chopped fresh lemongrass

1½ tablespoons Madras curry powder

2 cups finely chopped cauliflower

1 13.5-ounce can coconut milk

1 cup whole milk

Kosher salt and freshly ground black pepper

Juice of 2 limes (about ¼ cup)

¼ cup unsweetened dried coconut, toasted (optional)

2 tablespoons chopped scallions, for garnish (optional)

1 In a medium saucepan, heat the oil over medium heat. Add the onion, spring garlic, and lemongrass and sauté until softened but not colored, about 10 minutes. Add the curry and toast until fragrant, about 1 minute.

2 Add the cauliflower, coconut milk, whole milk, and 1 cup water. Bring to a simmer and cook until the vegetables are tender, about 20 minutes.

3 Puree the soup right in the pot with a hand blender. Season with salt and pepper and stir in the lime juice. Serve hot, topped with the toasted coconut or chopped scallions as a garnish.

SPICY COCONUT TEMPURA SHRIMP

This is a delicate, refined treatment for fried shrimp. The coconut milk adds a subtle sweetness to the tempura batter that in turn complements the shrimp. You can also use this batter to dip and fry thinly sliced vegetables.

■ **SERVES 4**

DIPPING SAUCE

¼ cup fish sauce

Juice of 3 limes (about 6 tablespoons)

2 tablespoons (packed) light brown sugar

1 teaspoon hot chile sauce, such as Sriracha

1 small shallot, finely diced

2 teaspoons grated peeled fresh ginger

1 to 2 Thai bird chiles, seeded and finely diced

2 tablespoons chopped fresh basil

2 tablespoons chopped fresh mint

SHRIMP

Canola oil, for frying

1 cup rice flour

⅓ cup cornstarch

1 teaspoon baking powder

¼ teaspoon cayenne

1 teaspoon kosher salt

1 large egg

½ cup chilled club soda or seltzer

1¼ cups chilled coconut milk

1 pound extra-large shrimp, peeled and deveined, tails on

1 To make the dipping sauce: In a medium bowl, whisk together the fish sauce, lime juice, sugar, chile sauce, shallot, ginger, and chiles. Stir in the basil and mint. Let sit at room temperature while you make the shrimp.

2 To make the shrimp: In a large straight-sided skillet, heat 2 inches of oil to 365°F. In a large bowl, whisk together the flour, cornstarch, baking powder, cayenne, and salt. In a spouted measuring cup, whisk together the egg, club soda, and coconut milk. Whisk into the flour mixture just until combined; a few lumps are okay, but don't overmix.

3 Dip the shrimp in the batter and fry, in 2 or 3 batches, until the coating is crisp and golden brown, about 4 minutes per batch. Drain on paper towels. Serve the shrimp immediately with the dipping sauce.

CURRIED COCONUT SOUP WITH LEMONGRASS AND SPRING GARLIC

COCONUT CUSTARD PIE

SPICY COCONUT TEMPURA SHRIMP

COCONUT CUSTARD PIE

The coconut flavor in this creamy custard really shines through— no need for whipped cream! This is one case where I would not use light coconut milk. The extra fat is needed here for a smooth and extra-rich custard.

■ **SERVES 8**

I 8-inch unbaked pie shell

I 13.5-ounce can coconut milk, stirred to combine

I cup whole milk

4 large egg yolks

¾ cup sugar

Pinch of kosher salt

¼ cup cornstarch

I tablespoon unsalted butter

I cup flaked sweetened coconut

1 Preheat the oven to 400°F. Line the pie crust with foil and fill with dried beans or pie weights. Bake until set but not colored, about 15 minutes. Carefully remove the foil and beans and bake until golden brown, about 10 minutes more. Cool completely.

2 In a medium saucepan, gently heat the coconut milk and whole milk until bubbles just begin to break the surface. In a large bowl, whisk together the egg yolks, sugar, and salt until smooth and lightened in color. Whisk in the cornstarch until completely smooth.

3 Pour in the milk mixture in a slow stream, whisking constantly, taking care not to add it too fast and scramble the yolks. Pour the mixture back into the saucepan and cook, stirring constantly, over medium heat until the mixture just begins to simmer (bubbles need to break the surface for the cornstarch to thicken). Immediately pour into a clean bowl and whisk in the butter.

4 Let cool for about 10 minutes and then lay a piece of plastic wrap or parchment directly on the surface. Cool to room temperature and then spread in the cooled pie crust. Chill until set, at least 4 hours or overnight.

5 Preheat the oven to 350°F. Scatter the coconut on a rimmed sheet pan and toast until golden, about 10 minutes, stirring once or twice. Cool. Sprinkle the toasted coconut on the finished pie just before serving.

ESPRESSO
INSTANT

14

While nothing beats a shot of fresh espresso in the morning, instant espresso powder is the way to go when you are cooking and want to enhance a dish with that unmistakable espresso flavor. Instant espresso, not to be confused with instant coffee, is actually dried espresso grounds that have been converted into powder. The powder dissolves immediately upon adding liquid.

Adding 1 or 2 teaspoons of instant espresso can highlight a chocolate recipe wonderfully. If you choose to add more than that when cooking, the coffee flavor will really come through and, in some cases, overpower other ingredients.

Tips

- Store espresso tightly closed in the pantry for up to one year, keeping it away from moisture.

- If espresso clumps, it's okay to scrape it with a fork.

- When buying espresso, choose an Italian brand for the deepest flavor.

ICED COFFEE WITH CARDAMOM

ESPRESSO CHEESECAKE

ESPRESSO BISCOTTI

ICED COFFEE WITH CARDAMOM

Cardamom is the world's third-most-expensive spice, after only saffron and vanilla, but a little goes a long way. It is extremely fragrant, with an aroma and taste all its own, and its notes pair perfectly with those of coffee. Adding this to a beverage such as iced coffee made with instant espresso is an easy way to impress your guests. ■ **SERVES 4**

Zest of 1 orange, removed with a vegetable peeler

2 tablespoons cardamom pods

⅛ teaspoon pure vanilla extract

½ cup instant espresso

½ to ¾ cup heavy cream

6 to 8 tablespoons sugar (optional)

Ice cubes

1 Bring 4 cups water to a boil in a small saucepan. Add the orange zest and cardamom and let steep, just below a simmer on low heat, to blend flavors, about 5 minutes. Add the vanilla and espresso, stirring to dissolve the crystals.

2 Strain into a pitcher and stir in cream (to your liking) and sugar (also to your liking, if using). Let cool to room temperature. To serve, pour into tall glasses filled with ice.

ESPRESSO BISCOTTI

You can serve these biscotti alongside coffee or espresso at the end of the meal or as a garnish for vanilla ice cream. The espresso notes marry perfectly with a vanilla-cream flavor. Stored in an airtight container, these biscotti will keep well for up to two weeks. ■ **MAKES ABOUT 3 DOZEN BISCOTTI**

2½ cups all-purpose flour

2 tablespoons instant espresso

1 tablespoon natural cocoa powder

½ teaspoon baking powder

½ teaspoon baking soda

¼ teaspoon salt

3 large eggs plus 1 large egg yolk

1 cup sugar

Finely grated zest of 1 small orange

½ cup slivered almonds

1 Preheat the oven to 350°F. Line a baking sheet with parchment paper. In a large bowl, stir together the flour, espresso, cocoa, baking powder, baking soda, and salt. In the bowl of an electric mixer fitted with the paddle attachment, mix the eggs and yolk and sugar on medium speed until thoroughly combined, about 1 minute. Add the flour mixture and mix just until a dough forms. Add the zest and almonds and mix just to combine.

2 Divide the dough in half and form into two 12-inch-long logs, about 3 inches apart, on the baking sheet. (If the dough is a little sticky, you can form the logs on a floured countertop.) Bake until puffed and cooked through, about 25 minutes. Remove from the oven and carefully move the logs to a cooling rack. Reduce the oven temperature to 325°F.

3 Let cool until you can handle the logs (they should still be soft to the touch), about 10 minutes. With a serrated knife, cut on a slight bias into ½-inch-thick biscotti. Arrange the biscotti on the baking sheet and bake until firm on the top side, 10 to 12 minutes. Flip them all and bake until the other side is firm, 10 to 12 minutes more. Cool completely on baking racks.

ESPRESSO CHEESECAKE

This cheesecake has a double shot of espresso flavor, in the crust and the filling, and the slight bitterness of the espresso cuts the rich creaminess of the cheese. For a smooth cheesecake with no lumps, it is very important to have the cream cheese at room temperature, so be sure to remove the cream cheese from the refrigerator one hour before you begin. This cheesecake can be made (and refrigerated) up to two days ahead of time. ■ **SERVES 8**

CRUST

10 to 12 Espresso Biscotti (opposite) or chocolate biscotti (store-bought is fine)

5 tablespoons melted unsalted butter

CHEESECAKE

4 ounces semisweet chocolate, chopped

¼ cup heavy cream

5 teaspoons instant espresso

1½ pounds cream cheese, at room tempterature

1 cup sugar

1 cup sour cream, at room temperature

3 large eggs, at room temperature

1 teaspoon pure vanilla extract

1 To make the crust: Preheat the oven to 350°F. In a food processor, grind the biscotti to crumbs, making enough to measure 1½ cups of crumbs. Pour the crumbs into a medium bowl and mix in the melted butter. Press the crust into the bottom of a 9-inch springform pan. Bake until the crust is set, about 15 minutes. Cool completely and reduce the oven temperature to 325°F.

2 To make the cheesecake: Set a metal bowl over a pan with 1 inch of simmering water. Add the chocolate and heavy cream and let the chocolate melt. When melted, stir in the espresso and let cool until just warm to the touch.

3 In the bowl of an electric mixer fitted with the paddle attachment, beat the cream cheese on medium speed until smooth. Add the sugar and beat until smooth, about 1 minute. Add the sour cream and beat to combine. Add the eggs one at a time and beat on high, scraping the bowl in between additions. Add the cooled chocolate mixture. Add the vanilla and beat on high until perfectly smooth, 1 to 2 minutes.

4 Pour the cream cheese mixture into the cooled crust. Bake until the cheesecake is set (the very center will be just a little bit jiggly), about 1 hour. Cool completely and then refrigerate until chilled before removing the ring of the pan.

15 FLOUR
ALL-PURPOSE

All-purpose flour is just that: all-purpose. Based on the amount of protein they contain, different flours produce different amounts of gluten, and all-purpose is right in the middle, so it is suitable for just about anything. A serious baker may also have pastry flour (less protein) or bread flour (more protein) in the pantry, but unless a recipe specifically calls for something else, all-purpose flour will do the trick.

All-purpose flour is the only flour I stock in my pantry at home. I prefer unbleached flour, as it hasn't gone through the chemical process used to whiten the flour, but either will work for these recipes. To measure flour, always scoop from the canister into the dry measuring cup and level with the back of a knife to get a consistent measurement.

Tips

■ Store in an airtight container.

■ All-purpose flour has had the germ and bran removed, so it is far less perishable than whole wheat flour and will keep in the pantry up to 8 or 9 months.

CRISPY CHICKEN PAILLARD

This method of cooking lightly floured chicken breasts over quick high heat results in a shatteringly crisp skin, but serve them as soon as you make them. I often choose this dish for my lunch and pair it with ripe tomatoes, bitter greens, and a bracing Chardonnay vinaigrette. ■ SERVES 4

4 skin-on, boneless chicken breasts
(each about 6 ounces)

Kosher salt

2 cups all-purpose flour

1 tablespoon smoked paprika

½ teaspoon garlic powder

½ teaspoon onion powder

Canola oil, for sautéing

4 tablespoons (½ stick) unsalted butter

4 sprigs fresh thyme

4 sprigs fresh rosemary

4 garlic cloves

1 Preheat the oven to 400°F. One at a time, put the chicken breasts between 2 sheets of plastic wrap and flatten to an even ½- to ¾-inch thickness with a meat mallet. Season the chicken with salt.

2 In a baking dish, stir together the flour, paprika, garlic powder, and onion powder. Season with salt. Dredge the skin side of the chicken breasts in the flour mixture.

3 Heat a large ovenproof skillet over medium-high heat. Depending on the size of the chicken breasts, you may need to use 2 skillets, and if so, simply divide the ingredients between the skillets and cook simultaneously. Add enough oil to film the bottom of the pan(s). When the oil just begins to smoke lightly, add the dredged chicken, skin side down, and shake the pan to make sure the chicken doesn't stick. Cook until the skin begins to brown, about 3 minutes.

4 Transfer the chicken to the oven and cook until the skin is very brown and crispy, about 5 minutes. Remove from the oven, flip the skin side up, and add the butter, thyme, rosemary, and garlic (or divide between the 2 skillets). Return to the oven and cook until the chicken is just cooked through, about 3 minutes. Drain the chicken on paper towels briefly before serving hot.

RICOTTA GNUDI
WITH MUSHROOM-GARLIC BUTTER

The light dusting of all-purpose flour on the outside of the raw gnudi is crucial to preserve the formed "dough" when cooking. These gnudi are also good with simple butter and cheese or a fresh marinara sauce. Use good-quality fresh ricotta from an Italian grocery or deli for the best results.

■ **MAKES ABOUT 2 DOZEN GNUDI, 4 TO 6 SERVINGS**

GNUDI

1 pound fresh ricotta, drained overnight

1 large egg plus 1 large egg yolk, beaten

½ cup chopped fresh chives

Finely grated zest of 1 lemon

Kosher salt

½ cup freshly grated Parmigiano-Reggiano

½ cup all-purpose flour, plus more for shaping

MUSHROOM-GARLIC BUTTER

2 tablespoons extra-virgin olive oil

8 ounces mixed wild mushrooms, such as any combination of porcini, chanterelle, and hen of the woods, wiped clean and broken into pieces or chopped

½ cup thinly sliced spring garlic, scallions, or spring onions (white and light green parts)

1 medium shallot, chopped

1 tablespoon chopped fresh thyme

½ cup chicken stock

3 tablespoons cold butter, cut into pieces

Splash of sherry vinegar

½ cup chopped fresh chives

½ cup freshly grated Parmigiano-Reggiano

Kosher salt and freshly ground black pepper

1 To make the gnudi: In a large bowl, combine the ricotta, egg and yolk, chives, lemon zest, and salt. Mix with a fork until smooth. Stir in the Parmigiano-Reggiano and flour until just combined. Don't overmix.

2 Spread a layer of flour on a rimmed sheet pan. Using 2 spoons, form the dough into about 24 oval-shaped gnudi, gently dropping them into the flour. Dust the tops with more flour and roll gently to coat. Refrigerate uncovered until firm, overnight if possible. When you are ready to cook the gnudi, bring a large pot of salted water to boil.

3 To make the mushroom-garlic butter: Heat a large skillet over medium-high heat. Add the oil. When the oil is hot, add the mushrooms. Let cook, without stirring, for a few minutes, until browned. Reduce the heat to medium, stir, and add the spring garlic, shallot, and thyme. Cook until the garlic greens are wilted, about 5 minutes.

4 Meanwhile, gently dust the excess flour from the gnudi and add them to the boiling water. Once the gnudi float, 2 to 3 minutes, simmer until cooked through, 4 to 5 minutes from the time they rise to the surface. Remove with a slotted spoon, reserving the pasta water, and add to the skillet with the mushrooms. Once all of the gnudi are in the skillet, add the stock, butter, and sherry vinegar, gently shake the pan, and stir until the sauce comes together, just 1 or 2 minutes, adding a little pasta water if the pan seems dry. Stir in the chives.

5 Off the heat, sprinkle with the cheese and stir gently to combine. Season with salt and pepper. Let the gnudi sit in the skillet for 1 minute to firm up and then serve.

CHICKEN
GUMBO

CRISPY
CHICKEN
PAILLARD

**RICOTTA GNUDI
WITH MUSHROOM-
GARLIC BUTTER**

CHICKEN GUMBO

A dark brown roux is essential to a good gumbo, so take your time when you brown the flour and oil mixture and stir often to keep it from burning. The flavor should be robust and nutty, a result of the browning process. ■ **SERVES 6**

4 slices thick bacon, chopped

6 chicken drumsticks

6 bone-in, skin-on chicken thighs

Kosher salt and freshly ground black pepper

2 links andouille sausage (about 8 ounces), diced

Canola oil

⅓ cup all-purpose flour

2 celery stalks, chopped (about ½ cup)

1 medium green or red bell pepper, cored, seeded, and chopped

1 medium onion, chopped (about 1 cup)

8 garlic cloves, finely chopped

1 tablespoon tomato paste

2 teaspoons chopped fresh thyme

¼ teaspoon cayenne, or to taste

½ cup dry white wine (optional)

6 cups chicken stock

2 dried bay leaves

4 ounces okra, trimmed and thinly sliced

1 tablespoon Worcestershire sauce

½ cup chopped scallions (white and green parts)

1 Cook the bacon until crispy in a large Dutch oven over medium heat. Remove and drain on paper towels. Season the drumsticks and thighs with salt and pepper. Raise the heat to medium high and brown the chicken in batches in the bacon fat, about 6 minutes per batch. Remove to a plate. Add the sausage and brown all over, about 5 minutes, then add to the plate with the chicken.

2 Add enough oil to the pot to make about ⅓ cup fat. Reduce the heat to medium and stir in the flour with a wooden spoon until smooth. Cook, stirring constantly, until the flour paste smells nutty and is a deep golden brown, about 15 minutes.

3 Add the celery, bell pepper, and onion and cook until slightly softened, about 3 minutes. Add the garlic, tomato paste, thyme, and cayenne and cook until the garlic is fragrant, about 1 minute. Add the white wine (if using) and bring to a boil. Whisk in the stock and bring to a simmer. Add the bay leaves and okra and return the chicken and sausage to the pot. Simmer briskly until the chicken is tender, about 45 minutes. Remove the bay leaves. Stir in the Worcestershire and reserved bacon, season with salt, sprinkle with the scallions, and serve.

GELATIN

Gelatin is a flavorless thickening agent derived from the collagen in various animal by-products. A small amount goes a long way: One package (2½ teaspoons) of gelatin will set 2 cups of liquid. Powdered gelatin must be bloomed before using. To do so, sprinkle the gelatin over some of the room-temperature liquid in the recipe, let sit until it dissolves, and then warm to melt it. Do not add gelatin to boiling liquid as the heat will destroy its setting ability.

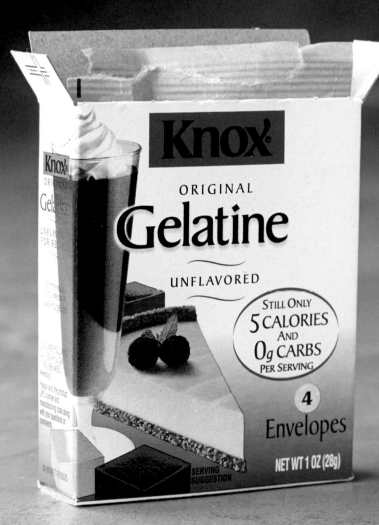

Tips

- Some recipes may call for sheet gelatin. One package of gelatin equals 3 or 4 sheets of gelatin in setting ability.

- Gelatin is not vegetarian. Agar-agar, made from algae, is a good vegetarian substitute and in powdered form can be used one for one in measurement.

PERFECT HERB MAYONNAISE

Just a small amount of gelatin makes this mayonnaise almost foolproof. If you've never made homemade mayo, this is a good recipe to begin with. A high-quality organic egg is important as the vibrant hue and taste of the yolk will add proper structure, depth of flavor, and beautiful color to the mayonnaise. ▪ **MAKES 2 CUPS**

½ teaspoon gelatin

I large organic egg plus I large organic egg yolk

I teaspoon dry mustard

I teaspoon sugar

I small garlic clove, minced

¼ cup chopped mixed soft herbs, such as any combination of Italian parsley, basil, chives, tarragon, and chervil

I½ to I¾ cups extra-virgin olive oil

Juice of ½ lemon (about I½ tablespoons)

I tablespoon white wine vinegar

Kosher salt and freshly ground black pepper

1 In a small bowl, sprinkle the gelatin over 2 tablespoons of cool water and let sit until absorbed, about 5 minutes. Put the bowl in a pan of hot water and stir to melt the gelatin.

2 In a blender or food processor, combine the gelatin mixture, the egg and egg yolk, mustard, sugar, garlic, and herbs and process until smooth. With the machine running, add the oil in a slow steady stream (just drips at first, adding more rapidly once the mayonnaise begins to thicken) to make a very thick mayonnaise. Stop and add the lemon juice and vinegar once the mixture begins to thicken and then add the remaining oil, stopping just before it has thickened to your liking. It will thicken a bit more once it is chilled.

3 Scrape into a small bowl, season with salt and pepper, and cover the surface with plastic wrap. Chill until ready to use. The mayonnaise will keep 3 or 4 days in the refrigerator, though the garlic flavor will intensify over time.

CLASSIC AMERICAN MEAT LOAF

The gelatin here holds the meat loaf together without overloading it with extra binders. It is juicy and tender when served hot but slices neatly when cold, almost like a pâté. So, try to save some for sandwiches the next day.

■ SERVES 6 TO 8

MEAT LOAF

2 tablespoons extra-virgin olive oil, plus more for the baking dish

½ cup finely chopped scallions (white and green parts)

¼ cup grated carrot

¼ cup finely chopped onion

I teaspoon dried thyme

I teaspoon ground cumin

½ teaspoon sweet paprika

½ teaspoon garlic powder

½ teaspoon onion powder

½ cup ketchup

2 teaspoons gelatin

2 pounds ground beef chuck

½ pound ground pork

2 large eggs, beaten

½ cup dried bread crumbs

Kosher salt and freshly ground black pepper

GLAZE

½ cup ketchup

I teaspoon Worcestershire sauce

½ teaspoon dry mustard

1 To make the meat loaf: Preheat the oven to 375°F. In a small skillet, heat the oil over medium heat. Add the scallions, carrot, and onion and cook until softened, about 10 minutes. Add the thyme, cumin, paprika, and garlic and onion powders. Cook until fragrant, about 1 minute. Scrape into a large bowl and let cool completely.

2 Meanwhile, heat the ketchup in the microwave until just warm to the touch. Sprinkle the gelatin over the ketchup and whisk to remove lumps. Add to the cooled vegetable mixture, then add the beef, pork, eggs, and bread crumbs. Season with salt and pepper and mix just until combined. Coat a 9 × 13-inch baking dish with oil and form the meat mixture into a loaf.

3 To make the glaze: In a measuring cup, stir together the ketchup, Worcestershire, and mustard. Brush a little glaze on the meat loaf and bake until the internal temperature reaches 160°F., about 1¼ hours, brushing three or four times with the glaze until you've used it all. Let the meat loaf rest at least 15 minutes before slicing.

BLACKBERRY PANNA COTTA

Panna cotta is a classic Italian dessert. Its simple base, consisting of cream, sugar, and gelatin, can be expanded upon in endless variations. Here I've added juicy blackberries, but it's also delicious made with raspberries or a combination of raspberries and blackberries. Although the gelatin is undetectable in the end result, it functions as a key ingredient in making the texture of this dessert work. With the correct balance of gelatin, the mouthfeel is creamy and not too firm. ■ **SERVES 6**

1³⁄₄ cups fresh blackberries

¹⁄₂ cup plus 2¹⁄₂ tablespoons superfine sugar

2¹⁄₂ teaspoons gelatin (I package)

3 cups heavy cream

I teaspoon pure vanilla extract

Fresh mint, for garnish

1 In a small bowl, toss the blackberries with ¹⁄₂ tablespoon of the superfine sugar. Let sit while you prepare the cream.

2 In a glass measuring cup, sprinkle the gelatin over ¹⁄₄ cup cold water. Let sit 5 minutes to dissolve. Put the cup in a pan of very hot water and stir to dissolve the gelatin.

3 In a medium saucepan, heat the cream and remaining ¹⁄₂ cup plus 2 tablespoons superfine sugar over medium heat, just until steaming, then stir to dissolve the sugar. Stir in the vanilla and dissolved gelatin. Let cool 15 minutes.

4 Divide the blackberries in the bottom of 6 glasses, reserving ¹⁄₄ cup for garnish. Pour the cream mixture over, cover with plastic wrap, and refrigerate until set, about 3 hours or overnight. Serve in the glasses, or dip glasses in hot water for about 10 seconds, then invert onto plates. Garnish with the remaining blackberries and mint sprigs.

CLASSIC AMERICAN
MEAT LOAF

PERFECT HERB
MAYONNAISE

BLACKBERRY
PANNA COTTA

17 HONEY

One of the oldest and most "natural" sweeteners, honey derives its flavor from the flowers on the specific plant the bees visit. Honeys range widely in color and taste—from acacia, which is very light and sweet, to buckwheat, which is richly flavored and almost as dark as molasses. Wildflower honey is from a mix of plants and is pretty utilitarian (clover honey, which is widely available, is also a good choice).

Honey can be stored at room temperature, but if exposed to humidity, it may crystallize in the jar. If this happens, put the jar in a bowl of warm water and let sit until the crystals dissolve. Honey is sweeter than regular sugar and is obviously moister, so they cannot be evenly swapped one for the other in baking. However, you can evenly substitute honey for half the sugar, reducing the total liquid in the recipe (this includes liquids and eggs) by one quarter for each cup of honey used.

Tips

■ Travel is a great way to expand your honey repertoire. Look for local honey from local bees at farmers' markets or food shops: It's a fun way to diversify your pantry a bit.

■ Plain honey, flavored honey, or even a piece of honeycomb is a great addition to a cheese tray set out for guests as an hors d'oeuvre or after a meal.

GOLD RUSH COCKTAIL

Honey, instead of simple syrup, is a great way to sweeten cocktails made with darker liquors, such as bourbon, rum, and whiskey. Although bourbon isn't to everyone's taste, the balance here among the sweet, acid, and liquor makes this a crowd-pleasing cocktail. This drink is our number-one cocktail at The Lambs Club in New York City, and I was lucky enough to learn it from the incredible bar man Sasha Petraske. *Merci, Sasha!*

■ **SERVES 4**

¼ cup honey

1 cup bourbon

3 ounces fresh lemon juice

1 In a small saucepan, warm the honey with 2 tablespoons water to make a syrup. Cool and chill completely, at least 2 hours.

2 In a cocktail shaker filled with ice, combine the chilled syrup, bourbon, and lemon juice. Shake vigorously until the contents are very cold, about 30 seconds.

3 Serve over large ice cubes in rocks glasses.

GOLD RUSH COCKTAIL

FROZEN HAZELNUT
AND HONEY TERRINE

FRESH RICOTTA
WITH HONEY AND LEMON

FRESH RICOTTA WITH HONEY AND LEMON

Use the least pasteurized, most natural milk and cream you can find to make fresh ricotta in order to expedite the curdling process. In the final dish, the honey balances the richness and acidity and is ultimately what makes honey, lemon, and ricotta such a classic and palatable combination.

■ SERVES 4

1 quart whole milk, preferably organic or not overly pasteurized

1 cup heavy cream, preferably organic or not overly pasteurized

Zest and juice of 1 lemon (about 3 tablespoons juice)

1 tablespoon white wine vinegar

¼ cup honey

Kosher salt or coarse sea salt

1 Prepare a double layer of cheesecloth over a fine sieve over a large bowl to catch the whey from the ricotta.

2 In a medium saucepan over medium heat, combine the milk and cream. Bring to just a simmer and stir in the lemon juice and vinegar and stir gently until the mixture curdles, about 30 seconds to a minute. Stir in the lemon zest. Let sit, off heat, for just 1 or 2 minutes, until the curds fully separate, and then gently pour into the cheesecloth-lined sieve.

3 Let the ricotta drain to the consistency you like, as little as 5 or up to 30 minutes, and then discard the whey in the bottom of the bowl. Let cool to room temperature.

4 Serve in small bowls. Drizzle with the honey and sprinkle with a little salt.

FROZEN HAZELNUT AND HONEY TERRINE

Honey and hazelnuts are a wonderful flavor pairing. You could also make this terrine with skinned almonds or walnuts or a combination of all three nuts. When serving a sweet frozen terrine, slice and serve on well-chilled plates with a dollop of unsweetened whipped cream on the side. ■ SERVES 6

½ cup hazelnuts

¼ cup honey

3 large egg whites, at room temperature

½ cup sugar

1 cup chilled heavy cream

¼ teaspoon pure vanilla extract

1 Preheat the oven to 350°F. Line an 8½ × 4½-inch loaf pan with plastic wrap that hangs 4 inches down the sides. Toast the nuts in a pan until light golden, shaking occasionally, 8 to 10 minutes. Cool completely.

2 Put the nuts in a food processor and grind until crumbly. Add the honey and process to a paste. Scrape into a large bowl.

3 In the bowl of an electric mixer fitted with the whisk attachment, whisk the egg whites on medium speed until foamy. Add the sugar in a slow stream and whisk on high speed for firm, glossy peaks, 1 to 2 minutes.

4 In a large bowl, whisk the cream to soft peaks and then stir in the vanilla.

5 Add about one third of the egg white mixture to the nut mixture and whisk to lighten it. Fold in the remaining egg white mixture to make a homogenous mixture. Gently fold in the cream, again until the mixture is homogenous. Spread into the prepared loaf pan. Smack the pan down on the counter to remove any air bubbles and smooth the top with a spatula. Cover the surface with the overhanging plastic wrap and freeze until solid, preferably overnight.

6 To serve, unwrap, and cut into slices with a warm serrated knife (warm a knife either under hot running water or over the stove flame for a few seconds).

JAM
RASPBERRY

Jelly, jam, and preserves are not all created equal and it is important to understand the differences. Jelly is made by straining out the juice of a fruit, making it smooth and sturdy. Jam is made by crushing the fruit, adding sugar, and incorporating all the chunky goodness into the end result. Preserves are whole pieces of fruit combined with a syrup or jam to "preserve" it. Therefore, jam, not too smooth and not too chunky, is a great choice to stock in the pantry because of its sweet-tart notes and versatility.

Many varieties of jam exist, but raspberry is a very straightforward choice. It marries well with several other cooking components such as chocolate, vanilla, citrus, tropical fruits, stone fruits, nuts, and ginger. If you start with a jam that is already a mixture of fruits and flavors, it would be more difficult to incorporate that into a successful dish.

Tips

- If a recipe calls for seedless jam and all you have is seeded, warm it over low heat in a small saucepan and then strain through a sieve.

- Try to avoid jams made with corn syrup as they are unnecessarily sweet.

- Once opened, jam can be kept in the refrigerator for up to 3 months.

RASPBERRY YOGURT

If you would like to serve flavored yogurts, it is incredibly easy to make them on your own! For variety, other fruit jams can be substituted for raspberry. ■ SERVES 4

1 cup raspberry jam

¼ cup sugar

2 cups 2% or whole milk Greek yogurt

1 tablespoon honey

Fresh raspberries, for garnish

1 Chill 4 small bowls or martini glasses or wineglasses for serving. In a small saucepan, combine the jam and sugar. Bring to a simmer over medium heat and cook, stirring, until the sugar dissolves. Scrape into a bowl and chill completely in the refrigerator, about 2 hours.

2 When chilled, whisk together the yogurt, jam mixture, and honey. Serve in the chilled bowls and garnish with raspberries.

RASPBERRY JAM TART

RASPBERRY YOGURT

**WATERMELON-
RASPBERRY
GRANITA**

WATERMELON-RASPBERRY GRANITA

Jam is an easy, efficient, and economical way to flavor granita. Freezers vary, so you may have to scrape your granita more (or less) often than the times noted here; just remember to scrape every time the ice crystals re-form around the edges of the pan. I prefer the tart flavor and texture of granita to ice cream and sorbet—and you don't need a fancy machine to make it! ■ SERVES 4 TO 6

½ cup raspberry jam

4 cups cubed seedless watermelon

Juice of ½ lemon (about 1½ tablespoons)

2 tablespoons superfine sugar, or more to taste, depending on the sweetness of your watermelon and brand of jam

1 In a small saucepan, heat the jam over low heat just until melted. Strain through a fine sieve to remove the seeds and cool to room temperature.

2 In a blender, combine the cooled jam, watermelon, lemon juice, and sugar. Blend until smooth. Pour into an 8 × 8-inch baking pan, preferably metal. Place in the freezer until ice crystals form around the perimeter, about 1 hour. Then scrape the crystals with a fork or spoon. Continue the scraping and freezing process (about every half hour) until all the granita has frozen and been scraped and you have a pan of light, pinkish ice crystals, 4 to 6 hours depending on your freezer. Gently scoop into chilled glasses and serve.

RASPBERRY JAM TART

Bake this tart with a sheet pan on the rack under it in the oven to catch the jam filling that might bubble over. When ready to serve, bring the tart right to the table as it is beautiful and will visually impress your guests. ■ **SERVES 8**

1¼ cups all-purpose flour, plus more for rolling the dough

1 tablespoon sugar

½ teaspoon baking powder

Pinch of kosher salt

¼ pound (1 stick) cold butter, cut into small cubes

2 large egg yolks

1½ cups raspberry jam

1 In a food processor, combine the flour, sugar, baking powder, and salt. Pulse to combine. Sprinkle in the butter and pulse in short bursts until the mixture is crumbly, with the largest pieces of butter about the size of peas. In a measuring cup, mix the egg yolks with 2 tablespoons cold water. Pour over the flour mixture and pulse a few times until a dough comes together, adding a little more water or flour as necessary until the dough sticks in a mass when pressed together.

2 Scrape the dough onto a floured counter and knead it a few times to bring it together. Flatten it into a disk, wrap in plastic, and chill at least 2 hours, or until firm.

3 Preheat the oven to 400°F. Remove the dough from the refrigerator 10 minutes before you're ready to roll. Once the dough has softened a little, cut off one third and set aside. Roll the larger piece of dough on a floured counter into an 11-inch round and fit it into a 9-inch tart pan with a removable bottom. Roll the remaining dough into a 10-inch round and cut it into strips about ½ inch wide.

4 Spread the jam in the tart shell. Lay half of the strips over the top in a row with even spaces in between. Lay the remaining strips over those, at a 45-degree angle. With your rolling pin, roll over the top of the tart to cut off any excess dough at the edges. Discard any excess dough.

5 Bake the tart until the jam is bubbly and the crust is golden, 35 to 40 minutes. Let cool to room temperature before slicing and serving.

19 KETCHUP

The H. J. Heinz Company began selling its genius condiment, ketchup, in 1876, and it seems like everyone in America has had a bottle in their fridge ever since. Beyond its traditional use for burgers, fries, and dogs, ketchup can add a concentrated burst of sweet and tangy flavor to stew and chili, and it is an especially great base for dips, sauces, and barbecue sauce.

Do not be afraid to embrace using ketchup to build off of in your cooking. It is not "cheating"—it is simply smart. Heinz ketchup is magnificent. This underrated staple is often relegated to the background as an assumed item, but you can doctor up bottled ketchup with herbs, spices, chiles, horseradish, capers, citrus zest, pickles, or a variety of other ingredients to make this old condiment taste fresh and new. The main components in most ketchups are tomatoes or tomato paste, vinegar, sugar (or corn syrup), salt, and spices. If you're concerned about high-fructose corn syrup in your diet, look for an organic ketchup, as that will usually be made with cane sugar, not corn syrup.

Tips

- Shake the ketchup bottle a bit to reincorporate the tomato water that rises to the top.

- See my "secret sauce" recipe for hamburgers on page 46 that uses ketchup as a base.

ULTIMATE COCKTAIL SAUCE

Cocktail sauce is a classic with shrimp, but I serve it with almost any kind of poached shellfish, as the ketchup base enhances the inherent brininess. It is also good to dollop on raw oysters. My recipe for cocktail sauce uses a fair amount of fresh horseradish, as it delivers a wonderful nasal heat and floral quality that you only get when grating it on the spot. ■ **MAKES ABOUT 1 CUP**

½ cup ketchup

¼ cup hot chile sauce, such as Sriracha

1 tablespoon prepared horseradish, drained

1 tablespoon grated fresh horseradish, or to taste

Juice of ½ lemon (about 1½ tablespoons)

2 teaspoons finely minced red onion

½ teaspoon Worcestershire sauce

Kosher salt and freshly ground black pepper

1 In a medium bowl, whisk together the ketchup, chile sauce, the prepared horseradish, the fresh horseradish, lemon juice, onion, and Worcestershire. Season with salt and pepper.

2 Refrigerate until well chilled. The cocktail sauce will keep up to 3 days, tightly covered, in the refrigerator. It may separate, so give it a quick stir again before serving.

BABY SHRIMP SALAD
WITH LETTUCE

This delicate shrimp salad can be thrown together in minutes for a light first course for a luncheon or summer dinner party. The ketchup here acts as the base for a tart, creamy, and slightly sweet dressing. ■ SERVES 4

1 ripe avocado

Juice of 1 lime (about 2 tablespoons)

¾ cup fresh cilantro leaves

Kosher salt

2 tablespoons crème fraîche

4 teaspoons ketchup

1 teaspoon prepared horseradish, drained

2 tablespoons chopped fresh chives

2 cups cooked baby shrimp or rock shrimp

16 pieces baby romaine or Gem lettuce, small leaves only, washed and dried

¼ cup chopped red onion

1 Halve and pit the avocado and scrape into a food processor. Add the lime juice, ½ cup of the cilantro leaves, and salt to taste. Process until smooth and spoon in the bottom of 4 rocks glasses or other small glasses.

2 In a medium bowl, whisk together the crème fraîche, ketchup, and horseradish. Stir in the chives. Add the shrimp and toss to coat with the sauce. Spoon into the glasses, over the avocado mixture. Stick the lettuce on the edges and sprinkle the top with the remaining cilantro and the onion.

ULTIMATE
COCKTAIL
SAUCE

KETCHUP-
GLAZED
CORNISH HENS

BABY
SHRIMP
SALAD
WITH
LETTUCE

KETCHUP-GLAZED CORNISH HENS

Ketchup is a good starting point for this BBQ-like glaze, but make sure to get the Cornish hen skin nice and crispy on the grill *before* you start brushing with the glaze, so the added sugars in the ketchup do not burn. ▪ SERVES 4

4 Cornish hens (each about 1¾ to 2 pounds)

Kosher salt and freshly ground black pepper

2 tablespoons extra-virgin olive oil, plus more for brushing

½ cup ketchup

2 tablespoons balsamic vinegar

Juice of ½ orange

1 garlic clove, finely chopped

1 teaspoon chopped fresh rosemary

¼ teaspoon crushed red pepper flakes

1 Preheat a grill to medium heat. Place 1 hen on the cutting board, breast side up, and with a large sharp chef's knife, cut out the backbone on both sides and cut off the wing tips (save for stock for another meal). Flip over the hen and trim a notch in the breastbone (the white piece of cartilage connecting the 2 breasts) to help flatten it. Flip the hen, breast side up again, and press to split the breast and flatten it. Repeat with the remaining hens. Season hens with salt and pepper and brush with oil.

2 In a small bowl, whisk together the ketchup, vinegar, the 2 tablespoons oil, the orange juice, garlic, rosemary, and pepper flakes. Set aside.

3 Grill the hens, breast side down, until the skin begins to crisp, then flip and grill breast side up for 10 minutes. Then flip and grill breast side down for 10 minutes more. A meat thermometer stuck in the thickest part of the thigh should read about 140°F. At this point, brush the hens liberally with the ketchup glaze. Once the glaze begins to set, 2 to 3 minutes, flip to breast side down again and glaze once more. Grill until the breast side is nicely lacquered, but not burned, 2 to 3 minutes, and then flip again. Brush with any remaining glaze and cook until the thermometer reads 165°F., 3 to 5 minutes more. Let the hens rest on a cutting board at least 5 minutes before serving.

MAPLE SYRUP

Vermont and Canada are the two largest producers of maple syrup, with Quebec being the largest exporter. In the cold northeastern winters, maple trees efficiently keep starch in their trunk, which in the spring thaw converts to sap. A tap is drilled into the side of the tree, a bucket is hung from the tap, and the sap runs out of the tap and into the bucket. After that, the sap is heated and reduced down into maple syrup. Upon production, maple syrup is graded, based on lightness of color and robustness of flavor. All are delicious in their own right, but lighter syrups work well on the table and darker syrups are used more often in cooking because of the deeper flavor.

Like honey, there are many different flavor nuances in syrup depending on the trees and where they are rooted. When traveling in the Northeast, I keep an eye out for local varieties, always picking up different bottles or jugs to keep on hand, as I tend to go through it quickly. The inherent golden caramel notes bring a well-balanced sweet quality to savory compositions and I like that it is so pure and natural.

Tips

- Once you open a container of maple syrup, keep it well sealed and in the refrigerator.

- If kept for a long time, maple syrup might crystallize on the bottom of the jug. As long as there is no mold present, it's still perfectly safe to eat.

MAPLE BUTTERMILK PORK ROAST

Pork and maple syrup have an excellent affinity for each other. The buttermilk and the caramel of the syrup will give the outside of the roast a beautiful color and the inside a lush flavor, in addition to keeping the meat moist. The leftover pork makes for an excellent base in a sandwich. Just add mustard, mayo, and red onion and serve between two pieces of country toast. ■ SERVES 4

PORK

1/2 cup pure maple syrup

2 cups buttermilk

4 sprigs fresh thyme

1 lemon, quartered

4 garlic cloves, crushed

2 fresh bay leaves

Kosher salt

1 4-bone pork loin roast
(3 to 3 1/2 pounds), tied

Freshly ground black pepper

Extra-virgin olive oil, for searing
the pork

Chicken stock, as needed (up to 2 cups)

SAUCE

2 tablespoons (1/4 stick) unsalted butter

1 large shallot, finely chopped

1 tablespoon all-purpose flour

Zest of 1 small orange, removed with
a vegetable peeler

1/4 teaspoon smoked paprika

2 fresh bay leaves

Splash of sherry vinegar

Kosher salt and freshly ground
black pepper

1 The day before you make the pork, combine the syrup, buttermilk, thyme, lemon, garlic, bay leaves, and 1 teaspoon salt in a large, sturdy resealable bag and add the pork. Marinate in the refrigerator overnight, turning the bag occasionally.

2 Preheat the oven to 425°F. Remove the pork from the marinade and let it come to room temperature while the oven preheats. Season the pork with salt and pepper.

3 Heat a large skillet over medium-high heat. Add a thin film of oil and sear the pork to brown on all sides, about 4 minutes in all. Transfer the pork to a rack in a roasting pan, but reserve the skillet. Roast the pork, bones up, for 15 minutes. Add 3/4 cup water to the pan and then reduce the oven temperature to 350°F. and roast until the internal temperature of the pork is 145°F., 40 to 45 minutes longer, adding up to another ¾ cup of water to the pan to keep the drippings in the bottom from burning. Let rest on a cutting board while you make the sauce. Pour the drippings into a bowl and remove the top layer of fat. Pour into a measuring cup and add enough chicken stock to make 2 cups in all.

4 To make the sauce: Over medium heat, heat the skillet used to sear the pork. Add 1 tablespoon of the butter and the shallot and cook until the shallot is softened, about 3 minutes. Sprinkle the flour over and stir to combine. Cook just 1 or 2 minutes and then add the orange zest and paprika. Pour in the stock, add the bay leaves, and bring to a rapid simmer. Simmer until slightly thickened and reduced by about one third, about 5 minutes. Remove the bay leaves, whisk in the remaining tablespoon of butter, and add a splash of sherry vinegar. Season the sauce with salt and pepper.

5 Carve the roast, between the bones, into 4 portions. Ladle about ¼ cup of sauce over each serving and pass the rest of the sauce at the table.

MAPLE BUTTERMILK PORK ROAST

GRILLED MAPLE-MUSTARD CHICKEN SKEWERS

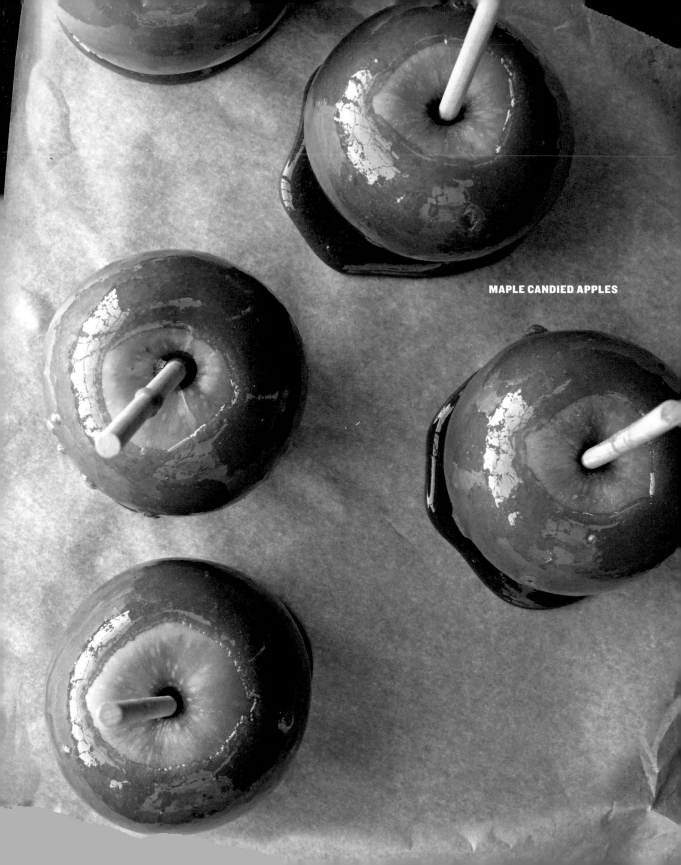

MAPLE CANDIED APPLES

GRILLED MAPLE-MUSTARD CHICKEN SKEWERS

Here the maple syrup rounds out the tartness of the mustard and yogurt and caramelizes the edges of the chicken on the grill. Do not marinate for more than two hours or the yogurt will begin to break down the chicken, resulting in a mushy texture. ■ SERVES 6

½ cup Dijon mustard

¼ cup pure maple syrup

¼ cup plain whole milk Greek yogurt

2 tablespoons extra-virgin olive oil

¼ cup chopped fresh cilantro

1 1-inch piece peeled fresh ginger, grated

¼ teaspoon ground allspice

Kosher salt and freshly ground black pepper

6 small boneless, skinless chicken breasts (about 2¼ pounds total), cut into 6 cubes each

2 tablespoons chopped fresh chives, for garnish

1 teaspoon poppy seeds, for garnish

1 In a large bowl, whisk together the mustard, syrup, yogurt, oil, cilantro, ginger, and allspice. Season with salt and pepper. Add the chicken cubes and toss to coat. Marinate in the refrigerator for 2 hours.

2 Preheat a grill to medium high. Soak 12 wooden skewers in water for 15 minutes, or use metal skewers. Drain the chicken from the marinade and stick 3 cubes on each skewer. Season with salt and pepper. Grill, turning on all sides to cook and caramelize the chicken evenly, about 8 minutes in all. Remove the skewers to a platter, and garnish with the chives and poppy seeds.

MAPLE CANDIED APPLES

Maple and apples are a classic combination on their own, but the other sugars and corn syrup are necessary to give the candy coating the perfect crackly crunch of an old-fashioned candy apple. Candy making can be finicky, so for best results, make this recipe on a cool, dry day. In the fall, bushels of farm-fresh apples are readily and economically available. This recipe is another way to put them to use besides pies and applesauce.

■ **MAKES 6 CANDIED APPLES**

1 tablespoon unsalted butter, plus more for the baking sheet

1 cup granulated sugar

1 cup (packed) light brown sugar

½ cup pure maple syrup

¼ cup light corn syrup

Pinch of kosher salt

6 Granny Smith or other tart apples

1 Line a baking sheet with a silicone baking mat or brush it with butter. In a medium saucepan, combine the granulated sugar, brown sugar, maple syrup, corn syrup, butter, and salt. Bring to a boil, without stirring, but gently shake the pan occasionally to make sure the sugar dissolves. Then stick in a candy thermometer and boil the syrup until it reaches 260°F. Immediately remove the pan from the heat and let it sit until the syrup thickens slightly, about 10 minutes.

2 Stick a Popsicle stick or chopstick in the top of each apple, and when the syrup is thick enough to thickly coat, dip each apple in the syrup. Swirl it around and tilt the pan to make sure each apple is coated almost all the way to the top. Let cool on the prepared baking sheet until hardened.

21 MILK
EVAPORATED

Evaporated milk is milk that has been reduced to remove excess water and then canned. It is shelf stable and ready to use as is. It comes in whole, low-fat, and fat-free varieties, though you are most likely to see the whole milk variety. Don't confuse it with sweetened condensed milk, which is also a canned dairy product but has added sugar, making it suitable only for sweet preparations.

Evaporated milk is good to use when you want the richness and creaminess of milk, but do not want to add a lot of extra liquid to your recipe.

Tips

- Evaporated milk will keep in the pantry for up to 2 years.

- Once opened, pour into another container, cover, and store in the refrigerator. Use leftovers within a couple of days.

CHUNKY ARUGULA AND HORSERADISH CONDIMENT

I recommend pairing this condiment with red meat, such as a grilled hanger steak, but it also works nicely with a piece of grilled chicken or grilled bread. ■ SERVES 6

3 cups packed baby arugula, washed and dried

½ cup macadamia nuts, toasted

¼ cup prepared horseradish, drained

2 tablespoons extra-virgin olive oil

2 tablespoons whole evaporated milk

2 tablespoons crème fraîche

2 tablespoons chopped shallots

Finely grated zest and juice of 1 lemon (about 3 tablespoons)

¼ teaspoon smoked paprika

Kosher salt and freshly ground black pepper

Combine the arugula, toasted nuts, horseradish, oil, evaporated milk, crème fraîche, shallots, lemon zest and juice, paprika, and salt and pepper in a food processor. Pulse to form a chunky but spreadable mixture. Season with salt and pepper.

WHITE ASPARAGUS SALAD

White asparagus is extremely labor intensive to grow and harvest. Its flavor is more woodsy than that of green asparagus, which has a slightly grassy taste. Poaching the white asparagus in milk helps maintain its color and adds an element of silkiness to the vegetable. Notes of orange, sesame, and vinegar bring the salad together and showcase this luxe ingredient in a deliciously elegant way. ▪ SERVES 4 TO 6

SALAD

1 bunch white asparagus (about 18 spears), trimmed, cut into 2-inch lengths

2 cups whole milk

½ cup whole evaporated milk

2 sprigs fresh thyme

1 dried bay leaf

2 cups fresh mandarin orange segments (from 2 or 3 oranges)

1 cup shaved fennel (from about 1 small bulb)

¼ cup fresh tarragon or Italian parsley leaves

Kosher salt and freshly ground black pepper

2 teaspoons toasted sesame seeds

DRESSING

½ tablespoon whole evaporated milk

1 teaspoon Dijon mustard

2 tablespoons champagne or white wine vinegar

⅓ cup grapeseed oil

1 To make the salad: In a medium saucepan, add the asparagus. Pour over the whole milk and evaporated milk so they just cover the asparagus. Add the thyme and bay leaf. Bring to a bare simmer and gently poach the asparagus until fork tender, 10 to 12 minutes, depending on their thickness. Drain, pat dry, and chill until cold, at least 1 hour.

2 To make the dressing: In a serving bowl, whisk together the evaporated milk, mustard, and vinegar. Whisk in the oil in a slow, steady stream to make a smooth dressing.

3 Add the chilled asparagus, oranges, fennel, and tarragon. Discard the bay leaf. Season with salt and pepper and toss to coat. Sprinkle with the sesame seeds, toss once more, and serve.

CHUNKY ARUGULA
AND HORSERADISH
CONDIMENT

WHITE
ASPARAGUS
SALAD

MALTED MILK SHAKE

MALTED MILK SHAKE

The use of malt, made of ground barley, adds a unique depth and taste to this milkshake. The choice of evaporated milk instead of regular milk ensures an extra-luscious end result. ■ **MAKES 2 LARGE OR 4 SMALL SHAKES**

1 pint good-quality vanilla ice cream
1 cup whole evaporated milk
1 cup crushed ice

¼ cup malt powder
1 tablespoon molasses

1 Combine the ice cream, evaporated milk, crushed ice, malt powder, and molasses in a blender and blend until thick and smooth.

2 Serve immediately in chilled glasses with straws and spoons.

MUSTARD
YELLOW

22

Mustard is a condiment made from whole, crushed, or ground mustard seeds with the addition of an acid (like vinegar or wine), salt, and flavorings. There is a wide range in color, texture, and flavor (from hot and spicy to very sweet), depending on how the seeds are ground and what is mixed in at the end. It gets its bright yellow color from the addition of turmeric and has a mild but tangy flavor. Yellow mustard is the most commonly sold mustard in the United States.

I keep this "ballpark" mustard, particularly French's, in heavy rotation because of its sharper and more peppery nose than other mustard varieties. It works to balance against a fatty meat, like hot dogs, pork, or sausage, but is also equally at home in the preparation of favorites like potato salad. Yellow mustard makes for a great emulsifier in creating a smooth vinaigrette and for whisking into a sauce at the end for an acidic tang and extra body. It is an incredibly versatile ingredient.

Tips

- Yellow mustard tends to separate in the bottle, so shake well before using.

- Unopened mustard will last up to 1 year in the pantry, but store in the refrigerator once you've opened it and then use within a few months.

HONEY-MUSTARD VINAIGRETTE

The sharpness of mustard on crisp green vegetables is a great combination. Vinaigrette can be strong, so cutting it with honey makes it palatable for a larger audience. This recipe works well on a salad or as a dipping sauce for seafood or my Family Chicken Fingers (page 70). This dressing will keep, well sealed, in the refrigerator for up to one week. If it separates, whisk to combine again before using. ■ MAKES ABOUT ¾ CUP

¼ cup cider vinegar

2 tablespoons yellow mustard

1 tablespoon honey

3 tablespoons grapeseed oil

3 tablespoons extra-virgin olive oil

1 teaspoon poppy seeds

Kosher salt and freshly ground black pepper

In a medium bowl, whisk together the vinegar, mustard, and honey until smooth. Slowly drizzle in the grapeseed and olive oils, whisking to form a smooth emulsion. Stir in the poppy seeds. Season liberally with salt and pepper.

DEVILED EGGS

When eggs are the star ingredient, I like to use the freshest, most flavorful ones available, so try to buy organic eggs and, if possible, from your local farmers' market. Yellow mustard is a good choice here for both color and flavor: It's not overly tart or bitter so it pairs well with the richness of the eggs and mayonnaise. ■ **SERVES 4 TO 6**

6 large eggs, preferably farm-fresh organic

2 tablespoons mayonnaise

1 tablespoon yellow mustard

2 dashes red Tabasco sauce

1 teaspoon finely minced shallots

Kosher salt and freshly ground black pepper

2 tablespoons chopped fresh chives

Sweet paprika, for garnish

1 Place the eggs in a medium saucepan and add water to cover. Bring to a boil and simmer gently, uncovered, for 10 minutes. Remove the eggs to a bowl of ice water to stop the cooking. When cooled, peel the eggs and halve them lengthwise. Carefully scoop the yolks into a medium bowl.

2 To the yolks, add the mayonnaise, mustard, Tabasco, and shallots. Mash with a fork until smooth. Season with salt and pepper. Mound the yolk mixture back into the whites with a spoon (or pastry bag for a more finished look). Garnish with chives and a sprinkle of paprika.

HONEY-MUSTARD
VINAIGRETTE

NEW ENGLAND
POT ROAST

DEVILED EGGS

NEW ENGLAND POT ROAST

The pot roast can be made a day ahead, but whisk in the mustard, horseradish, and parsley just before serving so the flavors stay bright.

■ SERVES 8 TO 10

1 beef chuck roast (about 3 pounds)

Kosher salt and freshly ground black pepper

3 tablespoons extra-virgin olive oil

2 carrots, cut into 2-inch chunks

3 celery stalks, cut into 2-inch chunks

2 medium onions, cut into 2-inch chunks

3 garlic cloves

3 sprigs fresh thyme

1 sprig fresh rosemary

2 dried bay leaves

¼ cup all-purpose flour

½ cup dry red wine

6 cups beef stock

1 pound red potatoes, cut into 2-inch chunks

¼ cup yellow mustard

2 tablespoons prepared horseradish, drained

¼ cup chopped fresh Italian parsley

1 Preheat the oven to 350°F. Season the roast with salt and pepper. In a large Dutch oven over medium-high heat, add the oil. When the oil is hot, add the roast and sear on all sides until well browned, about 5 minutes. Remove to a plate.

2 Add the carrots, celery, and onions and sauté until caramelized on the edges, about 5 minutes. Add the garlic, thyme, rosemary, bay leaves, and flour. Stir to incorporate the flour into the oil and cook until the flour smells toasty, about 2 minutes.

3 Pour in the wine and bring to a boil. Add the stock and roast back to the pot. Bring to a rapid simmer and cover tightly. Place in the oven and cook, covered, until the meat is just tender, about 2 hours. Add the potatoes, cover, and cook until the potatoes are done and the meat is tender (a knife will slide out easily with no resistance), about 30 minutes more. Remove the meat to a cutting board and let the sauce sit for a few minutes and spoon off any fat that has risen to the surface (or pour into a fat-separating measuring cup, pour off the fat, and add the sauce back to the pot).

4 Return the sauce to a simmer. Whisk in the mustard and horseradish and season with salt and pepper, if necessary. Stir in the parsley. Discard the bay leaves. Carve the meat into ½-inch-thick slices, against the grain, and serve with the sauce and vegetables.

OATS
STEEL CUT

23

Steel-cut oats are whole grain oats cut into pieces rather than rolled like the oatmeal most of us had growing up. Steel-cut oats have been the choice in Scotland and Ireland for ages, but they are finally getting attention here in America. They are nuttier and chewier than other types of oatmeal.

Although they can take up to 30 minutes to cook, you can shorten that cooking time if you soak them overnight in water in the refrigerator. I like to make a large batch of oats when I have time and then keep them in the fridge for a quick breakfast. Reheating is easy—just add a little water.

Tips

- Store steel-cut oats in your pantry in a tightly sealed container where they'll keep for up to 1 year.

- Previously cooked oats will keep for about 5 days in an airtight container in the refrigerator.

INTERNATIONAL EXHIBITION
1876
CERTIFICATE of AWARD
JOHN McCANN®
STEEL CUT
OAT MEAL
Group IV
UNITED STATES CENTENNIAL COMMISSION
(In accordance with the Act of Congress.)
PHILADELPHIA, September 27th, 1876.
John L. Campbell. Secretary.   A.T. Goshorn. Director General.   Jos. R. Hawley. President.
NET WT 28 OZ (1LB 12 OZ) 793g

OATMEAL COCONUT
CRUMBLE

OATMEAL, WALNUT, AND
SWEET GARLIC SPREAD

ULTIMATE
PORRIDGE

ULTIMATE PORRIDGE

Porridge, the original breakfast comfort food, is perfect in winter and a good vehicle to showcase other toppings, such as the dried fruit in this recipe. Nothing is more heartwarming to me than when I ask my family what they want for breakfast, and they proclaim "porridge!" I feel a great sense of purpose for the morning knowing that there is probably nothing healthier that I could invest my time in. Even when this porridge is simply drizzled with cinnamon and a bit of syrup, my family is asking for seconds. Three cups of milk makes a thick porridge, but use up to one cup more for a soupier result. While I prefer the richness of whole milk here, you can substitute 2% or fat-free as well. ■ **SERVES 4**

3 cups whole milk or more, to taste

Zest of ½ orange, removed with a vegetable peeler

3 tablespoons honey

¼ teaspoon ground ginger

Pinch of kosher salt

1 cup steel-cut oats

¼ cup dried cherries

¼ cup golden raisins

1 In a small saucepan, combine the milk, orange zest, honey, ginger, and salt. Bring to a simmer.

2 Put the oats in another small saucepan and ladle in half the warm milk. Bring to a simmer and cook until absorbed, about 8 minutes. Add the rest of the milk a ladle at a time, waiting for it to be absorbed before moving on (as if you were making risotto). The entire process will take 20 to 25 minutes, depending on the brand of oats you buy, ending up with a thick creamy porridge. If you want a slightly soupier porridge, stir in another ¼ cup or so of milk at the end. Discard the orange zest and serve the porridge in warmed bowls. Sprinkle each serving with some of the dried fruit.

OATMEAL, WALNUT, AND SWEET GARLIC SPREAD

This vibrant spread is best used on a yeasty country loaf with a good thick crust. It can be used for light open-faced tartines or in a bowl with toasted bread on the side for a cocktail party. The spread can be stored in an airtight container in the refrigerator for up to one week. ▪ **SERVES 6 TO 8**

1 head garlic

6 tablespoons extra-virgin olive oil

¼ cup steel-cut oats

Kosher salt

1 cup walnuts, toasted

1 teaspoon Dijon mustard

1 cup fresh Italian parsley leaves

Freshly ground black pepper

1 Preheat the oven to 375°F. Place the whole garlic head on a square of foil and drizzle with 1 tablespoon of the oil. Wrap up in the foil and roast until the garlic is soft and caramelized, 35 to 40 minutes. Let cool.

2 Meanwhile, bring ¾ cup water to a boil. Add the oats and a generous pinch of salt and simmer until cooked, 20 to 25 minutes, depending on the brand of oats you buy. Let cool slightly.

3 In a food processor, combine the walnuts, mustard, the remaining 5 tablespoons oil, the parsley, and a pinch of salt. Squeeze the garlic from the skins and add to the food processor. Pulse to make a chunky paste.

4 In a large bowl, stir the walnut paste into the oatmeal. Season with salt and pepper.

OATMEAL COCONUT CRUMBLE

This crumble is best served warm from the oven, but you can assemble it earlier in the day and pop it in the oven when your guests arrive to make things easier. Steel-cut oats give the topping a little more toothsome texture than regular rolled oats. ■ **SERVES 6**

7 tablespoons cold butter, cut into pieces, plus more for the baking dish

6 medium Golden Delicious apples, peeled, cored, and cut into 1-inch chunks

1 cup granulated sugar

Finely grated zest and juice of 1 lemon (about 3 tablespoons juice)

½ cup steel-cut oats

½ cup all-purpose flour

½ cup (packed) light brown sugar

¼ cup flaked sweetened coconut

¼ teaspoon ground cinnamon

Pinch of kosher salt

Classic Whipped Cream (page 233), for serving

1 Preheat the oven to 375°F. Butter a medium ovenproof pan or an 8 × 8-inch baking dish. In a medium saucepan, combine the apples, granulated sugar, lemon zest, and juice. Bring to a simmer and cook, stirring, just until the sugar melts. Pour into the prepared baking dish.

2 In a food processor, combine the oats, flour, and brown sugar. Pulse to grind the oats to small crumbles. Add the coconut, cinnamon, and salt. Pulse to combine. Add 6 tablespoons of the butter pieces and pulse until a crumble forms, with the largest pieces of butter the size of peas. Sprinkle the crumble over the apples and dot the top with the remaining 1 tablespoon butter. Bake until the topping is browned and the apple mixture is thickened and bubbly, about 35 minutes. Serve warm with whipped cream.

24 OIL
CANOLA

This all-American oil is derived from the rapeseed plant in a process that entails heating and then crushing the seeds. Stamped by the USDA as a heart-healthy oil that lowers cholesterol, it is a versatile cooking agent due to a high smoke point of 460°F., the temperature at which it would burn. (By contrast, butter and olive oil have low smoke points.)

Canola oil is ideal to cook with because of its neutral flavor. Unlike olive oil or other oils, such as nut oils, that have a discernible taste, canola oil can easily stay in the background carrying the other flavors of the dish.

Tips

- Canola oil is genetically engineered. If that is of concern, there are several brands of canola oil that are certified organic.

- Because of its high smoke point, canola oil is ideal for frying. After the second time using the oil for frying, you should discard it and start with fresh.

FRESH MOZZARELLA WITH BASIL OIL

This makes more oil than needed for the mozzarella—but it's hard to make a smaller amount of the oil. The leftover oil will keep in the fridge for three or four days and can also be used as a finishing oil for fish or chicken, on pasta or soup, or whisked into a vinaigrette. ■ **MAKES ABOUT 1 CUP OIL, 4 SERVINGS OF MOZZARELLA**

2 cups fresh basil leaves
½ cup fresh Italian parsley leaves
1 cup canola oil

1 ball fresh unsalted mozzarella, sliced (about 1 pound)
Pinch of kosher salt or coarse sea salt
4 small sprigs fresh basil, for garnish

1 Prepare a small bowl, set over another bowl of ice water, to cool the oil when it's ready.

2 In a blender, combine the basil, parsley, and oil and puree on high until the mixture feels just warm to the touch, 1 or 2 minutes. Immediately scrape the contents into the bowl and stir until cool.

3 The oil can be strained or served as is. To serve, fan the cheese onto plates, drizzle each piece with 1 or 2 tablespoons of the oil, and sprinkle with the salt. Garnish with the basil sprigs.

VEGETABLE
SOFFRITO TARTINE
WITH GOAT CHEESE-
YOGURT SPREAD

FRESH MOZZARELLA
WITH BASIL OIL

GARLIC
CROUTONS

VEGETABLE SOFFRITO TARTINE
WITH GOAT CHEESE-YOGURT SPREAD

Because the recipe yields more soffrito than you will need for the tartines, you can use the remainder as a condiment or as a base for pasta, tossed with a little pasta water and finished with grated cheese. It can be stored in the refrigerator for up to one week. ■ SERVES 4

SOFFRITO

⅓ cup canola oil

1 cup finely diced carrots

1 cup finely diced celery

1 cup finely chopped onion

½ cup finely chopped scallions
(white and green parts)

1 tablespoon finely chopped garlic

2 tablespoons tomato paste

4 large fresh basil leaves

Kosher salt and freshly ground
black pepper

GOAT CHEESE-YOGURT SPREAD

1 cup crumbled fresh goat cheese

½ cup whole milk Greek yogurt

1 tablespoon canola oil

2 tablespoons chopped fresh chives

2 tablespoons chopped fresh
Italian parsley

Kosher salt and freshly ground
black pepper

TARTINES

4 slices white bread, lightly toasted

¼ cup thinly sliced radishes

Coarse sea salt

1 To make the soffrito: Heat the oil in a saucepan over medium heat. Add the carrots, celery, onion, and scallions. Once it sizzles, reduce the heat as low as it will go and cook, stirring occasionally, until the vegetables begin to wilt, about 20 minutes. Add the garlic and cook over very low heat until fragrant, about 10 minutes.

2 Add the tomato paste and basil and season with salt and pepper. Continue cooking over very low heat, stirring occasionally, until the vegetables are very, very soft and the tomato paste has broken down into the oil, about 1½ hours.

3 To make the goat cheese–yogurt spread: In a mini food processor, combine the cheese, yogurt, and oil. Process until smooth. Scrape into a medium bowl and stir in the chives and parsley. Season with salt and pepper.

4 Spread the cheese–yogurt mixture on the toasted bread, layering soffrito on top of the cheese. Top with the radishes and season with salt.

GARLIC CROUTONS

The flavor imparted to the bread via these few simple steps will make it hard for you to buy store-bought croutons ever again. Once complete, the croutons will keep in an airtight container in the pantry for three or four days. ■ **MAKES 4 CUPS**

¼ **cup canola oil**

10 garlic cloves, crushed

4 cups bread cubes from a day-old loaf of country bread (can leave crust on)

Kosher salt and freshly ground black pepper

1 In a small saucepan, combine the oil and garlic and cook until the garlic sizzles and begins to soften but does not color, about 5 minutes. Turn off the heat and let steep for 1 hour. Pick out and discard the garlic.

2 Heat a large skillet over medium heat. Add the garlic oil. When the oil is hot, add the bread cubes and toss to coat. Cook until golden, toasted, and crisp, 12 to 15 minutes, adjusting the heat of the pan as you go if the bread is browning too quickly. Drain on a paper-towel-lined plate and immediately season with salt and pepper. Let cool before tossing in your favorite salad.

OIL
EXTRA-VIRGIN OLIVE

25

While there are many fantastic Italian olive oils, the United States, and particularly California, has caught up and is producing flavorful, nuanced olive oils. Olive oil is a very personal taste, so try a few to find one you like. They range from mild, fruity, and light yellow in color to grassy and peppery, and dark green, best for finishing a dish.

Look for "extra-virgin," cold-pressed oil for the purest flavor. Shaded glass bottles help protect the oil from sunlight, which breaks down the naturally occurring polyphenols and in turn shortens the shelf life. Olive oil is typically going to be more expensive than other cooking oils, but because of the crowded marketplace of this popular oil, you can competitively shop for a good one.

Tips

- Very expensive olive oil should not be used in cooking. Use it to drizzle on a finished dish or to dress a delicate salad.

- Though it's tempting, do not keep olive oil next to the stove for long-term storage. The heat from the stove will adversely affect the flavor.

OLIVE OIL POACHED COD

Poaching cod in olive oil enhances the creamy nature of the fish and helps cook it evenly and slowly so it does not dry out. The end result is luscious. Cod has a low fat content, and in other preparations, it can run the risk of drying out during cooking. As you will need quite a bit of olive oil for this recipe, a moderately priced brand from the grocery store will work just fine.

■ SERVES 4

3 cups extra-virgin olive oil

Zest of 1 lemon, removed with a vegetable peeler

4 sprigs fresh tarragon

2 dried bay leaves

½ teaspoon crushed red pepper flakes

4 skinless cod fillets (each about 6 ounces and 1½ to 2 inches thick)

Coarse sea salt and freshly ground black pepper

1 In a straight-sided sauté pan just large enough to hold the cod in 1 layer, combine the oil, lemon zest, tarragon, bay leaves, and pepper flakes. Heat over medium low until the oil reaches 200°F. on an oil/candy thermometer.

2 Season the cod with salt and pepper and gently place in the oil in a single layer, making sure the cod is completely submerged in the oil. Poach until just cooked through, 8 to 10 minutes, depending on the thickness of your fillets. Remove from the heat and let the cod cool in the oil for 5 minutes, to firm the fillets and make them easier to remove from the pan.

3 Remove the fillets with a slotted fish spatula and serve with a sprinkling of salt and pepper.

WARM TUNA SALAD

Poaching tuna awakens its natural flavors. It is essential to use a high-quality canned tuna packed in olive oil. Do not substitute tuna packed in water or even sushi-grade seared tuna. ▪ **SERVES 4**

12 ounces high-quality canned tuna in oil, such as **Ortiz**

2 tablespoons chopped fresh Italian parsley

¼ teaspoon crushed red pepper flakes

½ cup extra-virgin olive oil, plus more as needed

I cup halved cherry tomatoes

I cup sliced roasted red peppers, drained

½ cup chopped **Persian cucumbers**

½ cup thinly sliced red onion

¼ cup pitted and chopped **Cerignola** or other large olives

¼ cup chopped fresh basil

2 tablespoons capers, drained

¼ cup red wine vinegar

Kosher salt and freshly ground black pepper

1 Drain the tuna and empty it into a small skillet just big enough to hold it in 1 layer. Leave the tuna in big chunks; do not crumble. Sprinkle with the parsley and pepper flakes. Pour the olive oil over the tuna, so it just covers.

2 Heat the tuna over medium-low heat until warmed through, about 5 minutes, and then let it sit in the oil for an additional 5 minutes.

3 In a large serving bowl, combine the tomatoes, peppers, cucumbers, onion, olives, basil, and capers. Remove the tuna with a slotted spoon to the bowl. Drizzle with the vinegar and ¼ cup of the poaching oil. Season with salt and pepper and gently toss to combine, taking care not to break up the tuna too much.

**PIZZA MARGHERITA
WITH OLIVES AND ARUGULA**

WARM TUNA
SALAD

OLIVE OIL
POACHED COD

PIZZA MARGHERITA
WITH OLIVES AND ARUGULA

The no-cook sauce recipe here is especially quick and easy and can be used for any type of pizza or calzone you want to make. Use a mild olive oil to go with the sweetness of the sauce and balance the bitterness of the olives and arugula. ■ **SERVES 4 AS AN APPETIZER, 2 AS A MAIN COURSE**

1 cup canned **San Marzano** tomatoes with juice, crushed by hand

3 garlic cloves

5 tablespoons extra-virgin olive oil

Kosher salt

1 1-pound ball fresh pizza dough (can be purchased at your local pizzeria)

6 ounces fresh mozzarella, thinly sliced

10 fresh basil leaves

4 cups baby arugula, washed and dried

½ cup pitted and halved Niçoise olives

¼ cup thinly sliced red onion

1 tablespoon fresh lemon juice

Freshly ground black pepper

1 Preheat the oven to 450°F. with a pizza stone (or a flat baking sheet) on the bottom rack. In a small bowl, stir together the tomatoes, garlic, and 2 tablespoons of the oil. Season with salt. Let marinate at room temperature while the oven heats.

2 On a floured countertop, press and toss the dough into a 12- to 13-inch round. Put a piece of parchment paper on a pizza peel or flat sheet pan (this will help slide the pizza onto the stone). Place the round of dough on the parchment paper. Remove the garlic from the tomato sauce and spread the sauce on the pizza, leaving a 1-inch space around the crust. Top with the sliced cheese and roughly tear and scatter the basil on top. Drizzle with 1 tablespoon of the oil. Slide onto the heated stone and bake until the crust is golden and the cheese melted and bubbly, about 10 minutes.

3 While the pizza bakes, in a large bowl, toss together the arugula, olives, and onion. Drizzle with the lemon juice and remaining 2 tablespoons oil. Season with salt and pepper and toss.

4 When the pizza is out of the oven, let it sit for 1 minute and then cut into 8 slices. Top with the salad and serve.

PASTA
ELBOW MACARONI

26

Elbow macaroni are a classic American shape, seen on tables all over the United States in pasta salad and mac and cheese. However, elbows are thoroughly Italian, native to northern and central Italy, and they can be used in any pasta dish calling for a tube shape. Pasta that is tubular works with sauces that have bits and pieces; the idea is for the "extras" to get stuck inside.

Traditionally, elbows were used in Italian soups. I, however, prefer to use the elbows in untraditional ways, steering clear of the cliché dishes that have become synonymous with this pasta here in America. There are myriad combinations that work well with elbows; you just need to step off that road usually traveled. And if you can find them, ridged elbows can elevate your dish because the sauce clings to the outside ridges.

Tips

- You can substitute elbows in any recipe that calls for ziti, penne, or rigatoni.

- One or two handfuls of uncooked broken elbows can be added at the last minute to a vegetable soup, such as minestrone.

ELBOW MACARONI
WITH PINE NUTS, LEMON, AND FENNEL

The tart citrus combined with the fennel and the pine nuts takes me right back to a very special trip to Sicily, where I became engaged to my wife. We had the privilege of cooking and learning recipes in a local home, and I remember gazing across the kitchen at her thinking, *One day, hopefully, barefoot and pregnant.* . . . Even the slightest aroma from this dish and memories of my time on that special island come flooding back. Macaroni shells, a close relation to the elbow, can be substituted here as well.

■ SERVES 6

Kosher salt

I small fennel bulb, trimmed, cored, and thinly sliced

½ cup fennel fronds, coarsely chopped

½ cup toasted Mediterranean pine nuts

¼ cup chopped fresh mint leaves

Finely grated zest and juice of I lemon (about 3 tablespoons juice)

¼ teaspoon crushed red pepper flakes

¼ cup red wine vinegar

½ cup plus 2 tablespoons extra-virgin olive oil

3 cups elbow macaroni (about 12 ounces)

½ cup freshly grated Parmigiano-Reggiano

1 Bring a large pot of salted water to a boil.

2 In a serving bowl, combine the fennel and fronds, pine nuts, mint, lemon zest and juice, and pepper flakes. In a small bowl, whisk together the vinegar and ½ cup oil. Season the dressing with salt and pour over the fennel mixture. Let it sit while you cook the pasta.

3 Add the pasta to the boiling water and cook according to package directions until al dente. Drain, rinse, and pat dry on a sheet pan lined with a kitchen towel. In a large bowl, toss with the remaining 2 tablespoons oil.

4 Add the pasta to the fennel mixture and sprinkle with the cheese. Toss well and serve at room temperature.

ELBOW MACARONI WITH CRISPY BREAD CRUMBS AND BROCCOLI

ITALIAN PASTA SALAD

ELBOW MACARONI WITH PINE NUTS, LEMON, AND FENNEL

ITALIAN PASTA SALAD

This hearty salad makes a great lunch on a bed of greens and is also a wonderful addition to a buffet or antipasti spread. Try to make this salad only a few hours ahead or the cucumbers and tomatoes will release too much water into the dressing. ■ SERVES 6

Kosher salt

3 cups elbow macaroni (about 12 ounces)

½ cup plus 2 tablespoons extra-virgin olive oil

1 cup halved cherry tomatoes

1 cup diced English or Persian cucumbers

1 cup crumbled feta cheese

½ cup pitted and chopped Niçoise olives

½ cup diced salami

½ cup chopped roasted red peppers

¼ cup diced red onion

¼ cup chopped fresh Italian parsley

⅓ cup red wine vinegar

1 Bring a large pot of salted water to a boil. Add the pasta to the boiling water and cook according to package directions until al dente. Drain, rinse, and pat dry on a sheet pan lined with a kitchen towel. Toss with 2 tablespoons of the oil in a large serving bowl.

2 Add the tomatoes, cucumbers, cheese, olives, salami, peppers, onion, and parsley. Season with salt and toss to combine. In a small bowl, whisk together the vinegar and remaining ½ cup oil. Pour over the salad and toss well. Adjust the seasoning if need be. This salad is best if allowed to sit at room temperature for about 30 minutes before serving.

ELBOW MACARONI
WITH CRISPY BREAD CRUMBS AND BROCCOLI

Even the pickiest children will like this pasta. You can substitute cauliflower or peeled, diced winter squash for the broccoli, adjusting the cooking time accordingly. ■ SERVES 4 TO 6

Kosher salt

6 tablespoons extra-virgin olive oil, plus more for drizzling

½ cup panko bread crumbs

Finely grated zest of 1 lemon

2 tablespoons chopped fresh Italian parsley

3 cups elbow macaroni (about 12 ounces)

1 head broccoli, cut into small florets, about 4 cups

1 garlic clove, finely chopped

¼ teaspoon crushed red pepper flakes

1 cup chicken stock

1 cup freshly grated Parmigiano-Reggiano

1 Bring a large pot of salted water to a boil for the pasta. In a large skillet over medium heat, add 2 tablespoons of the oil. Add the bread crumbs and toast, stirring constantly, until the crumbs are crisp and golden, 4 to 5 minutes, taking care not to let them burn. Scrape the crumbs into a small bowl and toss with the zest and parsley and then season with salt.

2 Add the pasta to the boiling water and cook according to package directions until al dente, while you make the sauce. Wipe out the skillet used to toast the crumbs and return it to medium-high heat. Add the remaining 4 tablespoons oil, and when the oil is hot, add the broccoli and toss to coat. Sauté until it turns bright green, 2 to 3 minutes, and then add the garlic and pepper flakes. Cook until the garlic is fragrant, about 1 minute, and pour in the stock. Simmer until the broccoli is tender, 5 to 6 minutes.

3 When the pasta is done, scoop it out of the pasta water with a spider or small strainer and add directly to the sauce, reserving the pasta water. Simmer the pasta with the sauce, just to blend the flavors, 1 or 2 minutes more, and then drizzle with a tablespoon or so of oil and toss again.

4 If the sauce seems dry, add up to ½ cup pasta water. Off the heat, stir in the cheese. Serve in warmed bowls and sprinkle with the bread crumb mixture.

27 PASTA
ORECCHIETTE

Orecchiette is native to Puglia, the southern region that is the "heel" of Italy's boot. It takes its name, which means "little ear," from its round concave shape. The outside has ridges to grip the sauce and the indented side perfectly cups other ingredients in the dish, such as bits of sausage or pieces of vegetables.

Young diners really groove on the shape, as it is easy to stab with a fork and an entire piece can fit in a small mouth. It is also hard to overcook, making it well suited for multi-tasking at family dinnertime.

Tips

- Buy orecchiette that is made from 100% durum wheat semolina.

- Orecchiette can be substituted for any other shell-shaped pasta.

ORECCHIETTE WITH LEMON, GARLIC, AND PARMIGIANO-REGGIANO

This is a fairly simple and fast dish to make as the sauce takes the same amount of time to prepare as it does for the pasta to cook. I especially enjoy the heat that the crushed red pepper flakes add to this rich sauce, but if making this for children, you may want to reduce the pepper flakes by half or omit. ▪ **SERVES 6 TO 8**

Kosher salt

1 pound orecchiette

¼ cup extra-virgin olive oil

6 garlic cloves, crushed through a garlic press

1 teaspoon crushed red pepper flakes

1 teaspoon coarsely ground black pepper

1 stick (½ cup) cold unsalted butter, cut into small pieces

Finely grated zest and juice of 2 lemons (about 6 tablespoons juice)

½ cup freshly grated Parmigiano-Reggiano, plus more for serving

1 Bring a large pot of salted water to a boil. When thoroughly boiling, add the pasta and cook according to package directions until al dente.

2 While the pasta is cooking, make the sauce. In a large skillet or shallow Dutch oven, gently warm the oil over low heat. Add the garlic, pepper flakes, salt to taste, and the black pepper. When the garlic is soft and fragrant, but not colored, about 3 minutes, remove the pan from the heat and gently swirl in the butter until melted. Add the lemon zest and juice, stirring until slightly emulsified.

3 When the pasta is done, scoop it out of the pasta water with a spider or small strainer and add directly to the sauce, reserving the pasta water. Toss lightly with a large spoon, adding a little pasta water (about ½ cup in all) alternately with the cheese. Return to low heat briefly, just to simmer and bring the sauce together, and then serve immediately. Pass additional cheese at the table.

ORECCHIETTE
WITH SHRIMP,
PANCETTA, AND
FRESNO CHILES

ORECCHIETTE WITH
PARSLEY PESTO

ORECCHIETTE WITH
LEMON, GARLIC, AND
PARMIGIANO-REGGIANO

ORECCHIETTE WITH PARSLEY PESTO

Orecchiette is a splendid partner to any kind of pesto. I like to leave the pesto slightly chunky so the green flecks of parsley catch in the indentations in the pasta. ■ **SERVES 6 TO 8**

Kosher salt

¼ cup toasted pine nuts

3 garlic cloves, crushed

¾ cup extra-virgin olive oil

5 cups fresh Italian parsley leaves

½ teaspoon coarsely ground black pepper

Pinch of freshly grated nutmeg

½ cup freshly grated Parmigiano-Reggiano, plus more for serving

1 pound orecchiette

1 tablespoon unsalted butter, cut in cubes

1 Bring a large pot of salted water to a boil.

2 Add the pine nuts, garlic, and half of the oil to a food processor and pulse until just combined. Add the parsley, 1 teaspoon salt, the pepper, and nutmeg. Pulse, adding the remaining oil in a steady stream, scraping down the sides, to make a chunky paste. Add the cheese and pulse just to combine. (If making ahead, store now in the refrigerator in an airtight container and then bring to room temperature and stir before using.)

3 When the pasta water is thoroughly boiling, add the pasta and cook according to package directions until al dente. When ready to serve, drain the pasta, reserving about ⅓ cup pasta water. Add the hot pasta to a large serving bowl with the pesto, butter, and reserved pasta water. Toss until the butter melts and the pasta is coated with a glossy sauce. Serve immediately, passing additional cheese at the table.

ORECCHIETTE WITH SHRIMP, PANCETTA, AND FRESNO CHILES

Red fresnos are slightly hotter and sweeter than jalapeños and add a pop of color and sweet heat to this dish. But if you can't find them, substitute jalapeños. Cutting the shrimp in half allows them to cook faster and mix more thoroughly throughout the orecchiette. ■ **SERVES 6 TO 8**

Kosher salt

1 pound orecchiette

4 tablespoons extra-virgin olive oil

8 ounces pancetta, cut into medium dice

8 ounces large shrimp, peeled, deveined, tails removed, sliced lengthwise

2 garlic cloves, thinly sliced

½ teaspoon crushed red pepper flakes

2 fresno chile peppers, seeded and sliced into very thin rings

½ cup freshly grated Pecorino Romano, plus more for serving

½ cup roughly chopped fresh green or purple basil leaves

1 Bring a large pot of salted water to a boil. When thoroughly boiling, add the pasta and cook according to package directions until al dente.

2 In a large skillet or shallow Dutch oven over medium-low heat, heat 1 tablespoon olive oil and cook the pancetta to render the fat and crisp it, about 8 minutes. Remove to a paper-towel-lined plate to drain. Pour off and discard all but 1 tablespoon fat from the skillet. Raise the heat to medium and add 1 tablespoon of the oil. When the oil is hot, add the shrimp, garlic, and pepper flakes. Stir quickly and often so the garlic does not burn, 2 minutes at the most; the shrimp should be slightly undercooked.

3 Remove the shrimp to a warm bowl. Move the Dutch oven off the heat. Drain the pasta, reserving about ½ cup pasta water. Add the hot pasta to the skillet or Dutch oven and return to medium heat. Add the pancetta, shrimp, and reserved pasta water. Drizzle with the remaining 2 tablespoons oil. Toss and stir until the juices have combined and the shrimp is cooked through, about 3 minutes. Remove from the heat and add the chile peppers, cheese, and basil. Do not stir. Serve immediately, family style.

28 PASTA
SPAGHETTI

It is difficult for historians to pinpoint the exact origin of spaghetti, but there is pretty good evidence that Sicily was the birthplace and had a thriving spaghetti export business dating back to the twelfth century. Today, spaghetti with red sauce, meat sauce, or meatballs are truly universal dishes. These are undoubtedly satisfying, but I am always looking to push past the usual "default" dishes in an effort to explore what else can work for an ingredient.

Spaghetti is the best go-to for long pasta shapes. It is sold in three sizes: thin, regular, and thick. I use the regular for all the recipes here, as it cooks relatively quickly but is also forgiving. You do not need to watch it like a hawk to achieve that ideal al dente texture.

Tips

- Spaghetti can be substituted in other recipes that call for fettuccine, linguine, bucatini, or other long shapes.

- I like to sauté leftover cooked spaghetti in olive oil and add beaten eggs and grated cheese to make a pasta frittata.

SPAGHETTI WITH ANCHOVIES, RADICCHIO, AND SWEET ONIONS

This sauce is a study in how to balance flavors. The salty anchovy and the bitter radicchio hinge on the sweetness of the onions. Individually in the dish, none could work, but together they are a delicious combination.

■ **SERVES 4 TO 6**

Kosher salt

½ cup extra-virgin olive oil

1 medium sweet onion, sliced

1 pound spaghetti

2 small heads radicchio, cored and sliced (about 4 cups)

1 tablespoon chopped anchovies (about 3)

¼ cup chopped fresh Italian parsley

Finely grated zest of 1 lemon

2 tablespoons (¼ stick) unsalted butter (high-quality French butter preferred)

¼ cup freshly grated Pecorino Romano

Freshly ground black pepper

1 Bring a large pot of salted water to a boil. Heat a large skillet over medium heat. Add about one third of the oil. When the oil is hot, add the onion. Once the onion begins to cook, drop the pasta in the boiling water and cook according to package directions until al dente. Sauté the onion until softened, about 5 minutes, then add another one third of the oil and all the radicchio. Sauté until the radicchio wilts, about 2 minutes, and then add the anchovies, stirring to dissolve them into the oil. Ladle in about a cup of the pasta cooking water and bring to a boil. Simmer to reduce the sauce while the spaghetti finishes cooking.

2 When the pasta is done, remove with tongs and transfer to the simmering sauce, reserving the pasta water. Drizzle with the remaining oil. Add the parsley, lemon zest, and butter and toss to coat the pasta with the sauce, adding a little more pasta water if the sauce is dry. Off the heat, toss in the cheese and season with salt and pepper to taste.

SPAGHETTI WITH EGGPLANT AND RICOTTA SALATA

This classic simple Sicilian dish usually shows up in recipes with rigatoni. As you most likely will always have spaghetti on hand, it works just as well. If you can find smaller, less bitter Italian eggplants, there is no need to salt them first. ■ SERVES 4 TO 6

2 large eggplants (about 12 ounces each), cut in 1-inch chunks

Kosher salt

½ cup extra-virgin olive oil

4 garlic cloves, crushed

½ teaspoon crushed red pepper flakes

1 28-ounce can San Marzano tomatoes with juice, crushed by hand

1 pound spaghetti

2 cups roughly chopped fresh basil

½ cup freshly grated Parmigiano-Reggiano

4 ounces ricotta salata, shaved with a vegetable peeler

1 Put the eggplant chunks in a large colander in the sink and toss with 1 tablespoon salt. Let drain for 30 minutes. Rinse well and pat very dry.

2 Bring a large pot of salted water to a boil. Heat a large straight-sided skillet over medium-high heat and then add 3 tablespoons oil. Add half the eggplant and sauté until browned all over, about 4 minutes. Remove to a sheet pan lined with paper towels to drain and repeat with another 3 tablespoons oil and the remaining eggplant.

3 When the eggplant has browned, add the remaining 2 tablespoons oil to the skillet over medium-high heat. When the oil is hot, add the garlic and pepper flakes, and sauté until the garlic is fragrant, about 1 minute. Add the tomatoes and 1 cup of the salted boiling water. Bring to a simmer and add the eggplant. Simmer until the eggplant is tender and the sauce has thickened, about 15 minutes. Season with salt.

4 Cook the spaghetti until al dente. (The sauce can wait for the spaghetti but not vice versa.) Remove the spaghetti with tongs and add to the sauce, along with the basil. Toss to coat the pasta with the sauce.

5 Off the heat, sprinkle with the Parmigiano-Reggiano and toss well. Serve in a large pasta bowl with the shaved ricotta salata sprinkled over the top.

SPAGHETTI
WITH ANCHOVIES,
RADICCHIO, AND
SWEET ONIONS

SPAGHETTI
WITH EGGPLANT
AND RICOTTA
SALATA

SPAGHETTI
CARBONARA-STYLE

SPAGHETTI CARBONARA-STYLE

When making carbonara, it is essential to have all of your ingredients prepared and ready to go, and your guests seated at the table, as this dish is best served as soon as it is made. An escarole salad with the red wine vinaigrette on page 277 works perfectly served with this dish. ▪ **SERVES 4 TO 6**

Kosher salt

3 tablespoons extra-virgin olive oil

3 ounces slab bacon, cut into ¼-inch pieces

3 ounces pancetta, cut into ¼-inch pieces

1 pound spaghetti

1 small sweet onion, thinly sliced

3 garlic cloves, chopped

4 large egg yolks

1 cup freshly grated Parmigiano-Reggiano

¼ cup chopped fresh Italian parsley

1 Bring a large pot of salted water to a boil. Heat a large skillet over medium heat. Add the oil, bacon, and pancetta and cook, stirring, until the fat has rendered and the bacon and pancetta begin to crisp, about 3 minutes. Add the pasta to the boiling water and cook according to package directions until al dente. Add the onion and garlic to the skillet and cook until the onion is softened, about 5 minutes. Pour off all but about 3 tablespoons fat and add 1 cup pasta water. Bring to a simmer and cook to reduce by half to create a sauce.

2 In a medium bowl, whisk the egg yolks with ½ cup of the cheese. Temper the egg yolks by slowly whisking in about ½ cup pasta water.

3 When the pasta is done, remove with tongs and add to the sauce with the parsley. Toss to coat the pasta with the sauce. Remove from the heat and pour in the egg yolk mixture, tossing vigorously to cook the yolks and coat the pasta, without curdling the sauce. Taste for salt; it may not need any as the bacon and cheese are salty. Add the remaining ½ cup cheese, toss again, and serve immediately.

PEANUT BUTTER

Peanuts are native to the tropical regions of the Americas and Africa. Hundreds of years ago the Aztecs made the first version of peanut butter, a paste made from just peanuts. But peanut butter as we know it today has only been around and mass-produced for a little over a century.

   Commercial peanut butter is made by roasting, then grinding peanuts and combining them with sweeteners, salt, and stabilizers (to keep the natural oils from separating). "Natural" peanut butter has no stabilizers, which is why it has to be stirred before using.

Tips

- Natural peanut butters are great as a spread for toast and other uses right out of the jar, but for the recipes here, I use commercial peanut butter (with sugar) as it is a more consistent product for cooking.

- Peanut butter is best stored in the pantry at room temperature to stay spreadable. Once opened, it will keep for about 3 months. Natural peanut butters have a shorter shelf life because they don't have stabilizers, so use those within I month or keep refrigerated.

**SPICY PEANUT
BUTTER SLAW**

**BANANAS FOSTER
SMOOTHIE**

**PEANUT BRITTLE
ICE CREAM**

SPICY PEANUT BUTTER SLAW

Peanut butter provides the perfect foil for the crunchy vegetables in this slaw. And the inherent creaminess makes it a great substitute for the mayonnaise traditionally used in slaws. The thinner the veggies, the more they will soak up the delicious dressing. The dressing can be made one or two days ahead, but dress just an hour before serving for the best crunch. You could also add finely shaved jalapeños on top. ■ **SERVES 4 TO 6**

½ cup 2% Greek yogurt

¼ cup creamy peanut butter

¼ cup rice wine vinegar

2 teaspoons hot chile sauce, such as Sriracha

2 teaspoons dark sesame oil

1 teaspoon honey

Kosher salt

6 cups shredded green cabbage

1 cup julienned carrot

½ cup thinly sliced radishes

½ cup finely chopped scallions (white and green parts)

½ cup fresh cilantro leaves

½ cup golden raisins

1 In a medium bowl, whisk together the yogurt, peanut butter, vinegar, chile sauce, oil, and honey until smooth. Season with salt.

2 To the bowl, add the cabbage, carrot, radishes, scallions, cilantro, and raisins. Toss well to coat everything with the dressing. Refrigerate until chilled and toss again before serving.

PEANUT BRITTLE ICE CREAM

This makes more brittle than needed for the ice cream (extra will keep for one or two weeks). Store at room temperature in a sealed container, with parchment between the layers. ■ **MAKES ABOUT 1 QUART**

PEANUT BRITTLE

Cooking spray

1 cup sugar

¼ cup light corn syrup

1 tablespoon honey

½ pound (2 sticks) unsalted butter

3 cups roasted peanuts

½ teaspoon pure vanilla extract

ICE CREAM

2 cups heavy cream

1 cup whole milk

5 large egg yolks

⅓ cup granulated sugar

⅓ cup (packed) light brown sugar

½ cup creamy peanut butter

½ teaspoon pure vanilla extract

1 To make the brittle: Spray a silicone baking mat with cooking spray. In a saucepan over medium-low heat, combine the sugar, corn syrup, and honey. Once the mixture is warm, add the butter, stirring, until it melts. Add the peanuts and cook, stirring constantly so the edges of the pan don't burn, until the mixture is a dark golden brown, about 10 minutes.

2 Stir in the vanilla and immediately spread onto the baking mat with an offset spatula sprayed with cooking spray. Let cool completely and break into chunks. Finely chop enough brittle to yield ½ cup and set aside.

3 To make the ice cream: In a medium saucepan, bring the cream and milk just to a simmer. In a medium bowl, whisk together the egg yolks, granulated sugar, and brown sugar. Once the cream mixture has simmered, pour into the egg yolk mixture in a slow, steady stream, whisking constantly to avoid scrambling the yolks.

4 Pour the mixture back into the saucepan and cook, stirring constantly, until the mixture coats the back of a wooden spoon, about 5 minutes. Pour into a clean bowl and immediately whisk in the peanut butter and vanilla until smooth. Cool and refrigerate until chilled, at least 4 hours or overnight.

5 Churn in an ice-cream maker, according to the manufacturer's instructions, until soft set, adding the finely chopped peanut brittle at the very end and churning just to mix it through. Cover and freeze until scoopable. Serve with coarsely chopped brittle.

BANANAS FOSTER SMOOTHIE

Although peanut butter is not an ingredient in the traditional bananas foster dessert, it is a natural partner to all of the key ingredients—bananas, rum, and brown sugar. It also thickens the smoothie and adds a luxurious feel. You can omit the rum if making this smoothie for children. ■ **SERVES 4**

2 tablespoons (¼ stick) unsalted butter

¼ cup (packed) light brown sugar

4 ripe bananas, sliced

I tablespoon dark rum

I cup cold skim, low-fat, or whole milk

I cup non-fat, 2%, or whole milk Greek yogurt

⅓ cup creamy peanut butter

¼ cup sliced almonds, toasted

3 cups ice cubes

1 Chill 4 glasses in the freezer. In a large nonstick skillet, melt the butter over medium heat. Add the sugar and stir until bubbly and the sugar dissolves. Add the bananas and toss to coat. Cook, stirring, until the bananas are tender, about 2 minutes. Add the rum, remove from the heat, and transfer the contents of the skillet to a bowl to cool. Refrigerate until chilled.

2 In a blender, combine the cooled banana mixture, the milk, yogurt, peanut butter, almonds, and ice. Blend on high speed until smooth and creamy. Pour into glasses and serve.

30 PECANS

North America is the proud home of the pecan tree, part of the hickory family, and it can live to one thousand years old and grow up to one hundred feet tall. It bears a nut, also called pecan, with a hard exterior shell. The Native Americans originally named the pecan *pacane,* which translates to "nut to be cracked with a rock."

Pecans historically have been especially popular in the South, and you will find them in many traditional American baking recipes, but pecans are just as good in savory dishes. Their buttery richness is a great asset to more acidic ingredients, and they complement pork and poultry particularly well. Pecans can be purchased in halves or pieces. The halves are more expensive and are best used when appearance is key, as in Game Day Pecans (page 186). Otherwise, the pieces are a more economical option.

Tips

■ Because of their high oil content, pecans can go rancid quickly. If not using immediately, store in an airtight container in the freezer where they will keep for 6 to 9 months.

■ Ground pecans are a delicious addition to cookie crusts for cheesecake or pies. Substitute ½ cup ground pecans for the other crumbs in the recipe.

PECAN HERB PESTO

Pecans add a nutty sweetness to this pesto that you cannot get with pine nuts. This makes enough to sauce about 1 pound of your favorite pasta. When tossing pesto with pasta, reserve a little pasta cooking water to thin the sauce to your liking. ▪ **MAKES I GENEROUS CUP**

½ cup pecans

Finely grated zest of I lemon

I½ cups packed fresh basil leaves

I½ cups packed fresh Italian parsley leaves

I garlic clove

½ cup extra-virgin olive oil

¼ cup freshly grated Parmigiano-Reggiano

Kosher salt

1 Preheat the oven to 350°F. Scatter the pecans on a rimmed sheet pan and toast until they are fragrant and a shade or two darker, 7 to 8 minutes. Cool.

2 Put the pecans in a food processor with the lemon zest, basil, parsley, and garlic and pulse six or seven times to make a chunky paste. Scrape down the sides of the work bowl and, with the processor running, add the oil in a steady stream to make an almost smooth pesto.

3 Scrape the pesto into a bowl and stir in the cheese. Season with salt.

PECAN HERB PESTO

POMEGRANATE-GINGER SWEET POTATOES
WITH PECANS AND PUMPKIN SEEDS

GAME DAY PECANS

Sticky, sweet, and a little spicy, these nuts are great with a cold beer. They are best served warm, but not hot, from the oven. Of course, these work well for any cocktail gathering or bar setup, not solely on game day!

■ **MAKES 2 CUPS**

1 teaspoon kosher salt, plus more for sprinkling

½ teaspoon chili powder

½ teaspoon ground cumin

¼ teaspoon ground allspice

¼ teaspoon cayenne

¼ teaspoon ground cinnamon

¼ teaspoon sweet paprika

2 tablespoons (¼ stick) unsalted butter

¼ cup (packed) light brown sugar

1 tablespoon soy sauce

2 cups pecan halves

1 Preheat the oven to 325°F. In a small bowl, mix together the salt, chili powder, cumin, allspice, cayenne, cinnamon, and paprika. In a large skillet over medium-high heat, add the butter. When the butter is melted, add the sugar and soy sauce. Stir to melt and then stir in the spices.

2 Add the pecans and toss to coat them in the spiced butter. Cook and toss until the butter is absorbed into the nuts, 2 to 3 minutes. Spread on a rimmed sheet pan and bake until the nuts are fragrant and toasted and the coating is caramelized, 15 minutes. Let cool slightly on the sheet pan and serve warm.

POMEGRANATE-GINGER SWEET POTATOES WITH PECANS AND PUMPKIN SEEDS

A unique side dish, these super-food potatoes get children's taste buds exposed to a natural kind of sweet instead of artificial sugars, and adults are equally pleased to get in their nutrients in a tasty way as well. The sweet-tart pomegranate syrup can be drizzled on other roasted root vegetables as well—carrots, parsnips, and butternut squash, to name a few. ∎ SERVES 6

SYRUP

2 cups pomegranate juice

1 12-ounce can ginger ale

¼ teaspoon ground ginger

1 tablespoon unsalted butter

Kosher salt

SWEET POTATOES

3 sweet potatoes, peeled and cut into 1-inch chunks (about 2¼ pounds)

4 sprigs fresh rosemary

½ lemon, thinly sliced

3 tablespoons extra-virgin olive oil

Kosher salt

¼ cup coarsely chopped pecans, toasted

¼ cup pumpkin seeds, toasted

1 Preheat the oven to 400°F. To make the syrup: In a medium saucepan, combine the pomegranate juice, ginger ale, and ginger. Bring to a boil and simmer rapidly until reduced to ⅓ to ½ cup. The mixture should be syrupy and coat the back of a spoon. Whisk in the butter, season with salt, and keep warm.

2 To make the sweet potatoes: Toss the sweet potatoes with the rosemary, lemon slices, and oil on a rimmed sheet pan. Season with salt. Roast until the sweet potatoes are tender, tossing once or twice, 30 to 40 minutes. Toss with the pecans and pumpkins seeds and roast 5 minutes more. Mound the sweet potatoes on a platter and drizzle with the syrup, making sure you hit all of the potatoes.

31 PINE NUTS

Pine nuts are the edible seeds of the pine tree and are widely distributed both from China and from the Mediterranean. The labor-intensive harvesting process, which drives up the price, includes (in this order) gathering, roasting, and then cracking open the pine cones. Pine nuts are relatively small and have a creamy white color. The Mediterranean nuts are longer in shape and offer a more delicate flavor, whereas the Chinese nuts are shorter and less expensive. When possible, always opt for Mediterranean pine nuts, even though they are more costly, as their lineage and growing practices are safer.

When using pine nuts in a recipe, toasting ahead of time really brings out the flavor, so take the time to do that extra step. It is a little trick that can enhance the end result of your dish.

Tips

■ Toasting: Spread the pine nuts in one layer on a rimmed sheet pan. Toast in a 350°F. oven, shaking the pan intermittently, until light golden and fragrant, about 8 minutes. Watch carefully; once they start to toast, they can burn extremely fast.

■ Because of their high oil content, pine nuts go rancid quickly. If not using immediately after purchasing, store them in an airtight container in the freezer, where they will last up to 9 months.

PINE NUT AND POMEGRANATE SALAD

The pine nuts and pomegranates make this an exceptionally wonderful expression of a Mediterranean salad that is an interesting alternative to simple greens. Many gourmet stores now sell prepacked pomegranate seeds, which save a lot of mess and work. If frisée isn't available, you can substitute another slightly bitter green, like escarole, or even romaine.

■ SERVES 6

½ cup pine nuts

2 tablespoons red wine vinegar

1 teaspoon minced shallots

3 tablespoons extra-virgin olive oil

Kosher salt and freshly ground black pepper

1 tablespoon chopped fresh mint

4 cups torn frisée (about 1 medium head), washed and dried

1 cup pomegranate seeds

¼ cup freshly grated Parmigiano-Reggiano

1 Preheat the oven to 350°F. Scatter the nuts on a rimmed sheet pan and toast until lightly golden, about 8 minutes. Let cool.

2 In a large serving bowl, whisk together the vinegar and shallots. Whisk in the oil in a slow steady stream to make a smooth dressing. Season with salt and pepper. Whisk in the mint. Add the frisée, pomegranate seeds, and pine nuts. Toss to coat everything with the dressing.

3 Sprinkle with the cheese and toss to combine. Adjust the seasoning to taste and serve.

DIRTY RICE WITH PINE NUTS AND BLACK PEPPER

Here pine nuts give the rice crunch and texture. And dirty rice is the best way to use up what is left over in the fridge, too—a kind of catch-all for bits and pieces. Wild mushrooms can be substituted for the chicken livers and sausage to make this a lighter dish. ■ **SERVES 6 AS A SIDE, 4 AS A MAIN**

Kosher salt

1 cup wild rice

3 tablespoons extra-virgin olive oil

2 links hot Italian sausage
(about 5 ounces), casings removed

4 ounces chicken livers, trimmed and finely chopped

1 cup pine nuts

½ cup finely chopped onion

½ cup finely chopped celery

½ cup finely chopped green bell pepper

1 cup chopped scallions (white and green parts)

1 tablespoon chopped fresh thyme

½ teaspoon freshly ground black pepper

½ cup chicken stock

1 Bring a large pot of salted water to a boil. Add the wild rice. Simmer, uncovered, until the grains begin to split and the rice is tender but still a little chewy, 40 to 45 minutes (brands of wild rice differ in cooking times, so start checking after 30 minutes). Drain.

2 Meanwhile, in a large skillet over medium-high heat, add the oil. When the oil is hot, add the sausage. Cook and crumble with a wooden spoon until the sausage is browned all over, about 4 minutes. Add the chicken livers. Cook and stir until no longer pink, about 3 minutes. Add the pine nuts and toss to coat in the oil. Cook and stir until toasted, about 3 minutes.

3 Add the onion, celery, and bell pepper and cook until softened, about 7 minutes. Add the scallions, thyme, black pepper, and drained wild rice. Pour in the stock and cook until it is absorbed, about 3 minutes.

DIRTY RICE
WITH PINE NUTS
AND BLACK PEPPER

PINE NUT AND
OLIVE OIL GELATO

PINE NUT AND
POMEGRANATE
SALAD

PINE NUT AND OLIVE OIL GELATO

There is an inherent velvety nature to oil and with the high oil content in pine nuts, the two flavors seamlessly join together. When these savory items team up and are converted into a sweet and icy application, the taste in your mouth is beyond what you could ever expect. This gelato is fantastic on its own but also makes a great topping for sautéed figs or with a slice of flourless dark chocolate torte. ■ **MAKES ABOUT 1 QUART**

1 cup pine nuts	5 large egg yolks
2 cups whole milk	¾ cup sugar
1 cup heavy cream	Pinch of kosher salt
½ vanilla bean, split lengthwise	2 tablespoons extra-virgin olive oil

1 Preheat the oven to 350°F. Scatter the nuts on a rimmed sheet pan and toast until light golden, about 8 minutes. Let cool.

2 In a medium saucepan, combine the milk, cream, and ½ cup of the pine nuts. Heat over medium low until bubbles just form at the surface and then puree with a hand blender until smooth. Scrape in the seeds from the vanilla bean and add the pod. Bring to a bare simmer. In a large bowl, whisk the egg yolks with the sugar and salt until the yolks lighten in color and texture. Slowly whisk in the steaming milk mixture a little at a time, taking care not to add it too fast and scramble the yolks.

3 Pour the mixture back into the saucepan and cook, stirring constantly, over low heat until the custard thickens and coats the back of a spoon, 8 to 10 minutes. Immediately strain the custard through a fine sieve into a bowl. Whisk in the oil. Cool to room temperature, then chill the custard until cold, at least 2 hours or overnight.

4 Freeze in an ice-cream maker, according to the manufacturer's instructions, adding the remaining pine nuts at the end just to distribute them. The gelato will be soft, but ready to eat. For a firmer gelato, freeze for several hours after churning.

POPCORN
KERNELS

The popcorn we eat today is a type of corn specifically grown and dried to be popped, cultivated for just the right hull-to-kernel ratio. When heated, the kernel inside the hull expands and "pops" to make the fluffy exterior. People have been popping and enjoying kernels in the Americas for thousands of years: from ceremonial Aztec dances in the sixteenth century to pre–European invasion Native American feasts at Plymouth Rock. And, of course, today the movie industry has a thriving popcorn concession business. It is truly an indigenous food.

To make popcorn from plain kernels on top of the stove, heat a large deep pot over high heat with enough oil so its depth would cover a layer of kernels. When the oil is hot, drop in a few kernels. When they pop, add enough popcorn to make a single layer in the bottom of the pan and tightly cover, shaking the pot until you begin to hear popping. Once you hear two or three seconds in between pops, remove from the heat and let sit for I or 2 minutes to stop the popping. Shake the popcorn in a brown paper bag with melted butter and sea salt for a great snack.

Tips

- A quarter cup of unpopped kernels will yield about 8 cups of popcorn.

- Store unpopped popcorn in an airtight container in the pantry to keep it away from moisture, which will affect its ability to pop.

- For these recipes, don't use prepackaged popped popcorn.

SWEET AND SPICY
POPCORN

POPCORN
ICE CREAM

POPCORN SOUP

SWEET AND SPICY POPCORN

This popcorn is best served as soon as you make it. In a pinch, you can use natural flavored microwave popcorn as a base, but the clean, corny flavor of stovetop popcorn is best. ■ SERVES 4

3 tablespoons unsalted butter

¼ teaspoon cayenne

¼ teaspoon smoked paprika

¼ teaspoon five-spice powder

2 teaspoons (packed) light brown sugar

10 cups hot popped popcorn

Kosher salt

1 In a small saucepan, melt the butter over low heat and then add the cayenne, paprika, and five-spice powder. Stir and cook until the spices are fragrant, about 1 minute. Stir in the sugar it until dissolves.

2 Put the hot popcorn in a serving bowl. Drizzle the spiced butter over the popcorn, season with salt, and toss well. Serve immediately.

POPCORN SOUP

Depending on the power of your blender, you may want to strain this soup before serving to remove any stray kernels still floating around. Garnish with the popped popcorn at the very last minute, as it will dissolve as soon as it hits the hot soup. ▪ **SERVES 4**

3 tablespoons unsalted butter

2 medium leeks (white and light green parts), well rinsed and thinly sliced (about 1 cup)

2 garlic cloves, chopped

1 tablespoon chopped peeled fresh ginger

2 teaspoons curry powder

2½ cups popped plain popcorn

1 quart chicken stock

1 cup canned pumpkin puree

½ cup heavy cream

Juice of 1 lime (about 2 tablespoons)

Kosher salt

1 In a medium saucepan, melt the butter over medium heat. Add the leeks and cook until wilted, about 5 minutes. Add the garlic, ginger, and curry and cook, stirring, until fragrant, about 1 minute. Add 2 cups of the popcorn and toss to coat in the butter.

2 Add the stock, pumpkin, and cream. Bring to a simmer. Cook until the leeks are very tender and the popcorn has dissolved away from the kernels and the kernels are softened, about 20 minutes. The soup should have reduced by about one third.

3 Puree the soup with a hand blender or in batches in a countertop blender. Stir in the lime juice and taste for seasoning, adding a little salt if necessary. Serve in individual bowls with the remaining popcorn as a garnish.

POPCORN ICE CREAM

Similar to what we see with the Pine Nut and Olive Oil Gelato on page 192, this is another sweet application of a savory ingredient that yields sublime results. The milk and cream carry the buttery popcorn flavor, making the taste even more intense than that of eating freshly popped kernels. If time permits, make this ice-cream base and chill a full day before churning as the popcorn flavor will intensify as it sits. ▪ **MAKES ABOUT I QUART**

2 cups hot popped popcorn

I tablespoon unsalted butter, melted

Kosher salt

1½ cups whole milk

1½ cups heavy cream

6 large egg yolks

⅓ cup sugar

3 tablespoons light corn syrup

Cracker Jack or other sweet-coated popcorn, for garnish (optional)

1 In a medium, heat-proof bowl, toss the popcorn with the butter and sprinkle with salt. In a medium saucepan, heat the milk and cream to a simmer. Pour the milk mixture over the popcorn, and let steep for 30 minutes.

2 After 30 minutes, blend the popcorn mixture in a blender on high speed. Strain the mixture back into the saucepan and return to a simmer.

3 In a medium bowl, whisk together the egg yolks, sugar, corn syrup, and a pinch of salt. Once the milk mixture has simmered, pour into the egg yolk mixture in a slow, steady stream, whisking constantly to avoid scrambling the yolks.

4 Pour the mixture back into the saucepan and cook, stirring constantly, until the mixture coats the back of a wooden spoon, about 5 minutes. Pour into a clean bowl and refrigerate until chilled, at least 4 hours or overnight.

5 Churn in an ice-cream maker according to the manufacturer's instructions until soft set. Cover and freeze until scoopable. Serve topped with a garnish of Cracker Jack, if desired.

33 RAISINS
GOLDEN

Raisins are grapes that are dried in the sun, the shade, or an oven. With the exception of currants, all raisin varieties start from green grapes. Golden raisins generally come from the muscat grape and are oven-dried (rather than sun-dried) to retain their color. Golden raisins and other types of raisins can be used interchangeably in recipes, though I like the sweetness and amber color they add.

Great for baking or eating raw, raisins will keep for a month or two, tightly sealed, in a cool, dry place. After that, they're better off in the refrigerator, where they'll keep for up to 6 months.

Tips

- If the raisins harden when stored, put them in a small bowl, sprinkle with a little water, and microwave for 15 seconds to revive them.

- Combine golden raisins, salted almonds, and pumpkin seeds to make a quick snack mix. Store in an airtight container.

SUPERCHARGED GRANOLA

This flavor-packed granola will keep in your pantry in an airtight container for a week or two. It's good for breakfast with yogurt and fruit and also as a topping for ice cream. ■ **MAKES ABOUT 3½ CUPS**

1½ cups rolled oats (not instant)

½ cup whole skinned almonds, preferably Marcona, coarsely chopped

½ cup pecans, coarsely chopped

½ cup pistachios, coarsely chopped

2 tablespoons (packed) light brown sugar

2 tablespoons pure maple syrup

2 tablespoons extra-virgin olive oil

1 teaspoon chopped fresh rosemary

Kosher salt

¾ cup golden raisins

1 Preheat the oven to 250°F. In a large bowl, toss together the oats, almonds, pecans, and pistachios.

2 In a small saucepan, over low heat, stir together the sugar, syrup, and oil. Heat until the sugar is dissolved and then stir in the rosemary. Pour the mixture over the oats and toss well to coat. Lightly season with salt and toss again.

3 Spread on a rimmed sheet pan and bake until crispy and golden, stirring every 20 minutes, 60 to 75 minutes total. Cool, add the raisins, and toss well.

PARKER HOUSE ROLLS
WITH RAISIN GLAZE AND SESAME SEEDS

This raisin glaze can also be used on prebaked rolls if you don't feel like making them. Just brush the glaze on a package of small sweet rolls, sprinkle with the sesame seeds, and bake at 400°F. until heated through, about 4 minutes. ■ **MAKES 2 DOZEN ROLLS**

ROLLS

1 package (2¼ teaspoons) active dry yeast

¼ cup warm water (about 100°F., or just warm to the touch)

2 tablespoons plus a pinch of sugar

3 tablespoons unsalted butter, at room temperature

3 tablespoons shortening

1 cup whole milk

2 teaspoons kosher salt

1 large egg

4 cups all-purpose flour, plus more as needed

Olive oil, for greasing the bowl

3 tablespoons unsalted butter, melted and cooled

GLAZE

¾ cup golden raisins

1 teaspoon sesame oil

1 teaspoon honey

¼ teaspoon ground ginger

Kosher salt

1 tablespoon unsalted butter

1 tablespoon black sesame seeds

1 To make the rolls: In a spouted measuring cup, stir together the yeast, water, and a pinch of sugar. Let proof until bubbly, about 5 minutes.

2 In a medium bowl, melt the softened butter and the shortening together in the microwave. Whisk in the milk, the remaining 2 tablespoons sugar, and the salt. Let cool and then whisk in the egg.

3 Pour the yeast and milk mixtures into the bowl of a mixer fitted with the paddle attachment. Add the flour and beat on medium until a dough comes together. Switch to the dough hook and mix on medium high until a sticky dough forms, adding a little more flour or water, if necessary, so the dough forms a ball around the hook. Knead on medium-high speed until the dough is soft and smooth and cleans the sides of the bowl, about 4 minutes. Coat a large bowl with oil and turn the dough to coat in the oil. Cover lightly with plastic wrap or a kitchen towel and let rise at room temperature until doubled, about 1 hour.

4 Punch down the dough and cut into 2 equal pieces. On a lightly floured work surface, roll 1 piece out to about $\frac{1}{2}$ inch thick. Cut rounds with a 3-inch cutter, repeating with the remaining piece of dough and rerolling the scraps once to get about 2 dozen rounds.

5 With the dull side of a butter knife or a chopstick, make a slightly off-center crease in each round. Brush the surfaces with $1\frac{1}{2}$ tablespoons of the melted butter and fold the rounds over, along the crease, to make a semicircle with the bottom slightly overlapping the top. Arrange the rolls, not touching, on 2 baking sheets lined with parchment. Cover loosely with plastic wrap and let rise until doubled again, about 1 hour.

6 While the rolls rise, make the glaze: In a small saucepan, combine the raisins, 1 cup water, the oil, honey, ginger, and a pinch of salt. Bring to a boil and simmer until the liquid is reduced by about half and the raisins have softened, about 6 minutes. Let cool slightly. Puree in a blender with the butter to make a smooth glaze. Transfer to a bowl and set aside.

7 Preheat the oven to 425°F. When the rolls have risen, brush with the remaining $1\frac{1}{2}$ tablespoons melted butter and bake until just golden, 8 to 10 minutes. Remove from the oven, brush with the glaze, and sprinkle with the sesame seeds and a little salt. Bake just until the glaze is glossy and the undersides of the rolls are golden brown, about 2 minutes more. Cool on wire racks, but serve still warm from the oven.

VEAL RIB CHOPS WITH GOLDEN RAISIN SAUCE

Veal rib chops can be expensive, but combined with this easy raisin sauce they make a wonderful special-occasion meal. For a more everyday kind of meal, this sauce also pairs well with pork chops or chicken breasts.

■ SERVES 4

VEAL RIB CHOPS

2 tablespoons extra-virgin olive oil

4 veal rib chops (each about 12 ounces)

Kosher salt and freshly ground black pepper

RAISIN SAUCE

2 tablespoons unsalted butter

1 large shallot, diced

2 teaspoons chopped fresh rosemary

2 teaspoons chopped fresh sage

Finely grated zest and juice of ½ orange (about ⅓ cup juice)

1 cup chicken stock

2 teaspoons sherry vinegar

½ cup golden raisins

¼ cup capers, drained

1 tablespoon Dijon mustard

1 tablespoon chopped fresh Italian parsley

1 To make the veal chops: In a large skillet over medium-high heat, heat the oil. Season the veal chops with salt and pepper. When the oil is hot, brown the chops on both sides, 4 to 5 minutes per side. Remove the chops to a plate.

2 To make the raisin sauce: Wipe the skillet clean and return to medium heat. Add the butter, and when the butter is melted, add the shallot and cook until tender, about 5 minutes. Add the rosemary and sage and cook until fragrant, about 1 minute. Add the orange zest and juice and chicken stock and bring to a boil. Add the vinegar, raisins, and capers. Simmer until the sauce is reduced by half, about 3 minutes. Whisk in the mustard and parsley.

3 Return the chops to the sauce in the pan and then simmer until heated through and cooked to your liking, 2 to 3 minutes more. Spoon some sauce over each chop and serve immediately.

VEAL RIB CHOPS
WITH GOLDEN
RAISIN SAUCE

PARKER HOUSE
ROLLS WITH
RAISIN GLAZE AND
SESAME SEEDS

SUPERCHARGED
GRANOLA

34

RICE
LONG-GRAIN BROWN

Brown rice is white rice with the germ and bran still intact, making this grain a health food favorite because the germ and the bran contain most of the vitamins, minerals, and fiber. Those additional layers also add a chewiness and nutty flavor that you do not get from white rice. Because it is less processed, it is also more perishable than white rice.

To cook brown rice, bring I cup rice and 2½ cups water to a boil with a generous pinch of salt. Cover tightly and simmer until tender, 30 to 40 minutes. Let sit, covered, off the heat for IO minutes, then fluff with a fork.

Tips

■ For long-term storage, keep brown rice, tightly sealed, in the refrigerator to preserve the germ and bran.

■ If you soak brown rice in water for 30 minutes before cooking, you will get a fluffier grain, but your total preparation time will be longer. If you soak the rice first, when cooking you will use only 2 cups of water.

BROWN RICE PILAF

Because of its sturdy textural properties, brown rice is a little more forgiving and will be fine with an extra minute or two. Cooked brown rice should have a pleasant slightly al dente chew. ■ **SERVES 4**

¼ cup extra-virgin olive oil

I cup finely chopped bell pepper

I cup finely chopped carrot

I cup finely chopped onion

2 garlic cloves, finely chopped

2 teaspoons chopped fresh oregano

2 teaspoons chopped fresh thyme

I cup long-grain brown rice

2½ cups chicken stock

2 dried bay leaves

I cup chopped scallions (white and green parts)

2 tablespoons (¼ stick) unsalted butter, cut into pieces

Kosher salt and freshly ground black pepper

1 In a medium Dutch oven, heat the oil over medium heat. When the oil is hot, add the bell pepper, carrot, and onion and cook until they begin to soften, 7 to 8 minutes. Add the garlic, oregano, and thyme and cook until fragrant, about 1 minute.

2 Add the rice and stir to coat, toasting the rice in the oil, about 2 minutes. Add the stock and bay leaves and bring to a boil. Reduce the heat to a bare simmer and then cover and cook until the rice is tender but still a little chewy, about 45 minutes. Remove from the heat and let sit, covered, 10 minutes.

3 Uncover and fluff the rice with a fork. Add the scallions and butter and stir to combine and melt the butter. Remove the bay leaves and season with salt and pepper. Serve immediately.

BROWN RICE
CRAB CAKES

CREAMY RICE AND
MUSHROOM CASSEROLE

BROWN RICE
PILAF

BROWN RICE CRAB CAKES

Leftover brown rice helps stretch a pound of crab into eight good-size crab cakes. I get the best results with cooked rice that has first been spread on a plate and chilled in the refrigerator, which dries it out a bit. Depending on your preference, serve with Perfect Herb Mayonnaise (page 108) or Ultimate Cocktail Sauce (page 123) on the side. ■ **MAKES 8 CRAB CAKES**

1 pound jumbo lump crabmeat, picked over for shells

½ cup mayonnaise

¾ cup cooled cooked brown rice

½ cup chopped scallions (white and green parts)

1 large egg, beaten

Finely grated zest and juice of 1 lemon (about 3 tablespoons juice)

1 tablespoon chopped fresh tarragon

Kosher salt and freshly ground black pepper

1¼ cups fine dry bread crumbs, plus more as needed

Canola oil, for frying

1 lemon, cut into wedges, for serving

1 In a large bowl, combine the crab, mayonnaise, rice, scallions, egg, lemon zest and juice, and tarragon. Stir to combine. Season with salt and pepper. Sprinkle with ¼ cup of the bread crumbs and stir them in. You should be able to make a crab cake that just holds together but is still a bit wet. If the mixture is too wet to hold together (and it might be, depending on how wet the crab and cooked rice are), stir in up to ¼ cup more bread crumbs.

2 Form the mixture into eight 1-inch-thick cakes and put on a plate or platter. Refrigerate for 1 hour to firm them up.

3 When ready to cook the crab cakes, heat ½ inch oil in a large nonstick skillet and preheat the oven to 250°F. Spread about 1 cup bread crumbs on a plate and lightly dredge the crab cakes in bread crumbs. Fry the crab cakes in 2 batches until golden on both sides and heated through, 3 to 4 minutes per side. Drain the first batch on paper towels and keep them warm in the oven while you cook the second batch. Season the crab cakes with salt and serve with lemon wedges.

CREAMY RICE AND MUSHROOM CASSEROLE

Brown rice is nicely complemented with earthy flavors like mushrooms. This casserole makes a lovely light lunch or supper, paired with a simple green salad. ■ **SERVES 4 TO 6**

Kosher salt

1 cup long-grain brown rice

4 tablespoons (½ stick) unsalted butter, 2 cut into pieces, plus more for the baking dish

1 pound mixed mushrooms, such as any combination of button, cremini, shiitake, and oyster, sliced

Freshly ground black pepper

2 large eggs

½ cup whole milk

½ cup heavy cream

½ cup chopped scallions (white and green parts)

¼ cup chopped fresh Italian parsley

2 tablespoons chopped fresh tarragon

Finely grated zest and juice of ½ lemon (about 3 tablespoons juice)

½ cup crumbled fresh goat cheese

2 tablespoons fine dry bread crumbs

1 Preheat the oven to 350°F. In a medium saucepan, bring 2½ cups of water to a boil with a generous pinch of salt. When the water is boiling, add the rice, reduce to a simmer, cover, and let cook until the rice is just cooked, with still a little chew to it, 30 to 35 minutes. Remove from the heat and let stand, covered, for 10 minutes. Fluff with a fork and spread on a rimmed sheet pan to dry and cool.

2 In a large skillet over medium-high heat, melt 2 tablespoons of the butter. Add the mushrooms, season with salt and pepper, and cook, without stirring, until browned, about 2 minutes. Stir and cook until the mushrooms are well browned on both sides and no moisture remains in the pan. Transfer to a bowl to cool.

3 Butter an 8 × 8-inch baking dish. In a large bowl, whisk together the eggs, milk, and cream and then season with salt. Stir in the scallions, parsley, tarragon, and lemon zest and juice. Gently fold in the cooled mushrooms and the cheese, taking care not to break up the cheese much more. Pour the mixture into the prepared baking dish, sprinkle with the bread crumbs, and dot the top with the butter pieces. Bake until just set in the center, 35 to 40 minutes. Let cool for 10 minutes before serving.

35

RICE
LONG-GRAIN
WHITE

Rice is the single most ingested grain among the human population, and most of the rice eaten in America is long-grain white rice. Long-grain rice, when cooked properly, produces separate kernels that are fluffy yet dry. Short-grain rice, such as arborio, cooks up softer and creamier and is better for risottos and stewy dishes.

White rice is brown rice with the germ and bran (and many of the nutrients) removed and the kernels polished. It cooks more quickly and becomes fluffier than brown rice. Some rice, labeled as "converted," is steamed before milling, which adds back some of the nutrients but removes most of the flavor. Converted rice is also more expensive, so I suggest buying plain white rice. You can keep white rice, tightly sealed, in your pantry for up to a year.

Tips

- When cooking any type of rice, you can substitute chicken or vegetable stock instead of water to impart more flavor.

- When I cook rice for savory dishes, I always add a bay leaf to enhance the flavor.

CRISP SCALLOPS WITH CURRIED RICE FLOUR

In this recipe, you create your own rice flour and combine it with curry, a simple one-step way to crisp and flavor scallops. You can easily swap any other combination of spices you like for the curry to change up this recipe a bit—smoked paprika, cumin, and chili powder are all good choices. For the crispest result, make sure your scallops are very dry before dredging in the rice flour and coat them very lightly. ■ SERVES 4 AS AN APPETIZER

½ cup long-grain white rice

1 tablespoon curry powder

12 large sea scallops, side muscle or "foot" removed

Kosher salt

Canola oil, for sautéing

3 tablespoons unsalted butter

5 fresh thyme springs

Juice of ½ lime (about 1 tablespoon)

1 In an electric spice grinder or clean coffee bean grinder, grind ¼ cup of the rice with ½ tablespoon of the curry powder to a fine powder. Dump it into a shallow bowl and repeat with the remaining rice and curry.

2 Pat the scallops very dry and season with salt. Heat about ½ inch of oil in a large skillet over medium-high heat. When the oil is hot, dredge the scallops in the rice flour and add to the skillet; do not crowd them. (Depending on the size of your scallops, you may need to do this in 2 batches or use 2 skillets at once.) Let the scallops cook without moving them until the bottoms are crisp and browned, about 1½ minutes. Flip and brown the other side, about 1½ minutes. If your scallops are very large, you may also want to flip them on their rounded sides to brown for 1 minute more. When they're just cooked through, remove the scallops to warmed serving plates.

3 In a small skillet, melt the butter over medium heat. Add the thyme sprigs and cook until the milk solids in the butter begin to brown, about 2 minutes. Remove from the heat, stir in the lime juice, and season with salt. Drizzle the butter over the scallops and serve.

CRISP SCALLOPS
WITH CURRIED
RICE FLOUR

CHINESE-AMERICAN
FRIED RICE

MAPLE BROWN SUGAR
RICE PUDDING

CHINESE-AMERICAN FRIED RICE

This dish is a great use for leftover rice from Chinese takeout, but you can also make it from scratch. Start with 1½ cups uncooked rice to get the 3 cups needed for this recipe. I get the best results from rice that's been made ahead and chilled (it dries out a bit in the fridge). ■ SERVES 4

2 large eggs

Kosher salt

3 tablespoons peanut oil

3 slices thick bacon, coarsely chopped

1 medium red onion, thinly sliced

2 tablespoons finely chopped peeled fresh ginger

½ cup coarsely chopped roasted cashews

½ cup chopped fresh pineapple

3 cups cooked long-grain white rice (chilled leftover rice is preferable)

2 tablespoons soy sauce

¼ cup chopped scallions (white and green parts)

Hot chile sauce, such as Sriracha, for serving (optional)

1 In a small bowl, beat the eggs with a pinch of salt. Heat a large nonstick skillet over medium-high heat. Add 1 tablespoon of the oil. When the oil is hot, pour in the eggs and quickly rotate the skillet to evenly cover the bottom with egg. Cook just until the eggs set, 1 to 2 minutes, then flip out onto a cutting board to cool. Roll up the cooled egg pancake and cut into shreds.

2 Return the skillet to medium heat and add the bacon. Cook until the bacon is crisp, about 4 minutes, and then remove the bacon to paper towels to drain. Discard the bacon fat.

3 Return the skillet to medium-high heat. Add the remaining 2 tablespoons oil. When the oil is hot, add the onion. Cook and stir until the onion is crisp-tender, 2 to 3 minutes. Add the ginger and cook until fragrant, about 1 minute. Stir in the cashews and pineapple to combine and then add the rice. Sprinkle with the soy sauce and raise the heat to high. Cook and stir just until combined and the rice is heated through, 1 to 2 minutes. Stir in the scallions, omelet shreds, and bacon and serve with chile sauce, if desired.

MAPLE BROWN SUGAR RICE PUDDING

Here is one occasion on which it's okay to overcook rice! In fact, that is exactly what you want to do in order to make this rice pudding soft and creamy, like that old-style diner favorite. I add a little milk to the cooking water to make the rice extra creamy. ■ **SERVES 6 TO 8**

I quart whole milk

I cup long-grain white rice

Kosher salt

I vanilla bean, split lengthwise

2 large egg yolks

I large egg

¾ cup (lightly packed) light brown sugar

¼ cup pure maple syrup

2 tablespoons cornstarch

¼ teaspoon freshly grated nutmeg

Classic Whipped Cream (page 233), for serving

1 In a medium saucepan, bring 2 cups water and 2 cups of the milk to a simmer. Add the rice and a pinch of salt. Simmer, uncovered, until the rice is very, very tender, about 30 minutes. Strain in a colander and rinse briefly with cold water, letting the rice cool to room temperature.

2 In another medium saucepan, add the remaining 2 cups milk. Scrape in the seeds from the vanilla bean and add the pod. Bring the milk to a simmer.

3 In a large heat-proof bowl, whisk together the egg yolks, egg, sugar, syrup, cornstarch, and nutmeg. Slowly pour in the hot milk, whisking constantly and taking care not to scramble the eggs. Once all the milk has been added, pour it back into the saucepan and return to medium-low heat. Cook, stirring constantly, until just a few bubbles appear (do not boil) and the mixture has thickened. Immediately remove from the heat and pour into a bowl. Remove the vanilla pod, cover the surface with plastic wrap or parchment paper, and chill for 1 hour.

4 When chilled, fold the rice into the custard and refrigerate until very cold, at least 2 hours. Serve in small bowls or glasses, with a dollop of whipped cream on top.

SOY SAUCE

36

Soy sauce is made by fermenting soy beans, wheat flour, water, and salt. The most premium soy sauces are fermented naturally and some cheaper soy sauces add corn syrup. Soy sauces are labeled "light" and "dark," referring to whether they were taken from the top (light) or bottom (dark) of the barrel after fermentation. There are variations within both categories, too, but for most uses, light soy is the way to go and will work well in these recipes. It has a clean, salty flavor with a hint of sweetness and is thinner than dark soy sauces.

I often use soy sauce as a secret ingredient in my home cooking, sneaking it into vinaigrettes. Its floral saltiness coupled with its inherent dark caramel bitterness can easily rev up a sauce or vinaigrette. It adds a wonderful rich deep flavor without overpowering the main ingredient, allowing for an impressive and sometimes undetectable layering of tastes, similar to the way anchovies or Worcestershire sauce can work in a dish.

Tips

- Once opened, soy sauce will keep for about 6 months, tightly sealed, in the pantry or refrigerator.

- If making a recipe with soy sauce, always taste before adding salt.

STEAMED BROCCOLI
WITH SOY VINAIGRETTE

This dressing would be great on just about any steamed green vegetable. It can also work well as a base for an Asian-inspired slaw with cabbage, carrots, scallions, and julienned snow peas. ▪ **SERVES 4**

BROCCOLI

1 large head broccoli

SOY VINAIGRETTE

1 large egg yolk

1 tablespoon fresh lemon juice

1 tablespoon sherry vinegar

1 tablespoon soy sauce

1 teaspoon Dijon mustard

¼ cup canola oil

Kosher salt and freshly ground black pepper

1 To make the broccoli: In a large pot, bring 1 inch of water to a boil and fit with a steamer basket. Trim the bottom inch or so from each large piece of broccoli (there should be 2 or 3 large stalks in a head) and cut each stalk lengthwise into quarters. Arrange the broccoli in the steamer and tightly cover the pan. Steam until tender, about 12 minutes, depending on the thickness of the stalks.

2 To make the vinaigrette: In a blender, combine the egg yolk, lemon juice, vinegar, soy sauce, and mustard and blend until smooth. With the blender running, pour in the oil in a steady stream to make a smooth, thick vinaigrette. Transfer to a bowl and season with salt (if necessary) and pepper. If the vinaigrette is too thick, thin with 1 or 2 teaspoons of water.

3 Arrange the hot cooked broccoli on a platter and drizzle with the dressing or serve on the side as a dipping sauce.

MUSHROOM SOY TURKEY BURGER

Turkey burgers are generally tough to execute because turkey has a low fat content, which, in turn, makes most turkey burgers quite dry and bland. Ground turkey is not suited for burgers on its own. However, the soy-mushroom mixture here boosts the ground meat by adding moisture and flavor, providing for a delicious alternative to red meat. ■ SERVES 4

2 tablespoons extra-virgin olive oil, plus more for brushing the grill

4 cups finely chopped white or cremini mushrooms

1/4 cup finely chopped red onion

2 garlic cloves, chopped

2 tablespoons soy sauce

1 1/4 pounds ground turkey

1 large egg, beaten

1/4 cup fine dry bread crumbs

Kosher salt and freshly ground black pepper

4 brioche buns, split and toasted

4 thick slices of ripe tomato

4 lettuce leaves, washed and dried

1 In a medium skillet over medium-high heat, add the oil. When the oil is hot, add the mushrooms and cook, without stirring, until the undersides are browned, 2 to 3 minutes. Let brown on the other side, about 2 minutes, and then reduce the heat to medium and add the onion and garlic. Cook and stir until the onion is softened, about 5 minutes. Remove from the heat, stir in the soy sauce, and cool.

2 In a large bowl, combine the turkey, egg, bread crumbs, and cooled mushrooms. Season with salt and pepper. Mix together lightly with your hands, just to combine, but don't overmix. Form into 4 patties, each about 1 inch thick. Refrigerate while you preheat the grill.

3 Preheat a grill to medium high (the burgers can also be done in a grill pan or skillet on the stovetop). Brush the grill grates with oil and grill the burgers until nicely marked and cooked through, about 4 minutes per side. Serve on the buns with tomato and lettuce.

LAMB KEBABS
WITH SPICY HERB AND SOY MARINADE

The savory qualities of the soy cut through the gaminess of the lamb and make it almost sweet. To stretch this to serve more guests, skewer squares of onion and bell pepper between the lamb cubes. If you double the marinade, you could also use it for a whole boneless and butterflied leg of lamb. ■ **SERVES 4 TO 6**

½ cup soy sauce

½ cup fresh basil leaves

½ cup fresh cilantro leaves

½ cup fresh mint leaves

½ cup coarsely chopped shallots

1 1-inch piece peeled fresh ginger, coarsely chopped

2 tablespoons honey

1 tablespoon dark sesame oil

1 tablespoon hot chile sauce, such as Sriracha

Juice of 2 limes (about ¼ cup)

2 pounds boneless leg of lamb, trimmed of fat and sinew and cut into 1½-inch cubes

2 tablespoons chopped fresh basil

2 tablespoons chopped fresh cilantro

2 tablespoons chopped fresh mint

1 In a blender or food processor, combine the soy sauce, basil leaves, cilantro leaves, mint leaves, shallots, ginger, honey, oil, chile sauce, and lime juice. Blend until smooth. Pour into a nonreactive bowl or baking dish and add the lamb cubes, tossing to coat in the marinade. Cover and marinate in the refrigerator for 4 hours or as long as overnight.

2 Preheat a grill or grill pan to medium high and oil the grill grates. Soak 12 wooden skewers in water for 15 minutes, or use metal skewers. Divide the lamb among the skewers, putting 3 cubes per skewer. Pat off any excess marinade. Grill the skewers, turning on all sides, until the lamb is done to your liking, 8 to 10 minutes for medium rare to medium. Scatter the chopped basil, cilantro, and mint on top of the skewers just before serving.

MUSHROOM SOY
TURKEY BURGER

STEAMED
BROCCOLI
WITH SOY
VINAIGRETTE

LAMB KEBABS
WITH SPICY HERB AND
SOY MARINADE

STOCK
CHICKEN

Classic chicken stock, one of the main staples in American cooking, is made from simmering chicken bones, onions, carrots, celery, thyme, parsley, and peppercorns in a large pot of water and then straining the liquid after cooking it for several hours. While that is still the optimal way to go, I also always keep purchased stock on hand for when I need a quick burst of concentrated chicken flavor or simply do not have the time to make a batch from scratch.

Chicken stock is the ultimate base for soups, stews, and all things braised or moist-roasted. When purchasing prepared stock, I prefer the cartons over the cans (a better value and, I think, a cleaner taste). Look for lower-sodium, lower-fat varieties without MSG.

Tips

■ Freeze stock in ice-cube trays to add to sauces on the fly.

■ Unopened, the cartons will keep for I year in the pantry, or longer—look at the expiration date. Once opened, transfer to a nonreactive container, refrigerate, and use within 3 or 4 days.

CHICKEN SOUP

After completing this recipe, you can recycle the chicken carcass to make another round of soup stock for another day. To do this: Cover the carcass in a pot with more stock (or just water), add a handful of chopped carrot, celery, and onion, and simmer until flavorful, sixty to ninety minutes. Leftover soup will keep in the refrigerator for three or four days or in the freezer for several months. ■ **SERVES 6**

I chicken (about 3 pounds), trimmed of excess fat

3 quarts chicken stock, or as needed

I cup diced carrot

I cup diced celery

I cup thinly sliced leek (white and light green parts)

¼ cup white wine

5 sprigs fresh thyme

3 dried bay leaves

½ teaspoon dried oregano

Kosher salt

I cup fresh peas or frozen peas, thawed

Snipped fresh dill, for garnish (optional)

1 Rinse the chicken well and put in a pot large enough to leave 1 or 2 inches of space between the chicken and the walls of the pot. Add chicken stock to cover. Bring to a boil and then gently simmer until the chicken is tender throughout, 60 to 75 minutes, skimming and discarding the foam from the top as you go. Remove the chicken to a bowl and let cool. Pull the chicken meat from the carcass, discarding the skin. Chop or shred the chicken meat into bite-size pieces.

2 Skim any foam and fat from the top of the chicken broth and discard. Return the stock to a simmer. Add the carrot, celery, leek, wine, thyme, bay leaves, and oregano. Season with salt. Simmer until the vegetables are tender, about 20 minutes.

3 Add the peas and reserved chicken meat. Simmer until the peas are tender, about 10 minutes. Discard the bay leaves. Sprinkle with fresh dill, if desired, and serve hot.

PENNE WITH CHICKEN, PANCETTA, AND CRISPY SHREDDED LETTUCE

CHICKEN SOUP

NEW ENGLAND
CLAM CHOWDER

NEW ENGLAND CLAM CHOWDER

While it may be more common to use water or fish stock to make this type of soup, I prefer using chicken stock, as it has a level of gelatin from the bones of the chicken used to make it. Although a small amount, it really pulls the soup together. You could use canned clams and bottled clam juice here, but I think it is worth the effort to use fresh clams. Ask your fishmonger to shuck the clams for you and save the shucking juices. Strain the juices through cheesecloth before using to remove grit and pieces of shell. ■ SERVES 6

3 tablespoons extra-virgin olive oil

3 slices bacon, chopped (about ½ cup)

1 cup chopped onion

1 cup chopped celery

1 tablespoon chopped fresh thyme

¼ cup all-purpose flour

1 quart chicken stock

1 cup clam juice

2 dried bay leaves

2 medium russet potatoes (about 1 pound), diced

1½ cups chopped shucked clams

¾ cup heavy cream

Kosher salt and freshly ground black pepper

2 tablespoons chopped fresh Italian parsley

Lemon wedges, for serving

Oyster crackers, for serving

1 Heat a large Dutch oven over medium heat. Add 1 tablespoon of the oil and the bacon and cook until crisp, about 4 minutes. Drain on paper towels and discard the bacon fat.

2 Add the remaining 2 tablespoons oil to the pot. Add the onion, celery, and thyme. Cook, stirring occasionally, until the onion is softened, about 8 minutes. Sprinkle the flour over the vegetables and stir to coat the vegetables. Cook until the flour smells toasty but not browned, about 3 minutes. Pour in the stock, clam juice, and 1 cup water and add the bay leaves. Bring to a simmer and add the potatoes. Simmer until the potatoes are tender, about 15 minutes.

3 Add the clams and cream and return to a simmer. Cook until the clams are tender, about 5 minutes more. Season with salt and pepper and stir in the bacon and parsley. Remove the bay leaves. Serve with lemon wedges and oyster crackers.

PENNE WITH CHICKEN, PANCETTA, AND CRISPY SHREDDED LETTUCE

You might not think of using iceberg lettuce in a pasta, but it adds just the right amount of crunch and sweetness here. The chicken stock reduces to a savory glaze that works perfectly with the slightly sweet lettuce. This pasta is quick and surprisingly kid-friendly. ■ SERVES 4 TO 6

Kosher salt

3 tablespoons unsalted butter

4 ounces diced pancetta (about ¾ cup)

12 ounces penne

1 cup chopped scallions (white and green parts)

3 garlic cloves, finely chopped

Pinch of crushed red pepper flakes

2 cups leftover diced boneless, skinless cooked chicken

1 cup chicken stock, plus up to 1 cup more as needed

Finely grated zest and juice of ½ lemon (about 1½ tablespoons juice)

½ head iceberg lettuce, washed and shredded (about 4 cups)

¼ cup coarsely chopped fresh mint

¼ cup coarsely chopped fresh Italian parsley

¾ cup freshly grated Parmigiano-Reggiano cheese

1 Bring a large pot of salted water to a boil for the pasta. In a large skillet over medium heat, melt 1 tablespoon of the butter and add the pancetta. Cook until the pancetta renders its fat, about 4 minutes. If there is more than 2 or 3 tablespoons of fat in the skillet, spoon off the excess and discard.

2 Once the pancetta is rendered, add the pasta to the water and cook according to package directions until al dente. Raise the skillet heat to medium high and add the scallions, garlic, and pepper flakes. Cook, stirring, until the scallions are wilted, about 3 minutes. Add the chicken, 1 cup chicken stock, and the lemon zest and juice. Bring to a boil and add the lettuce. Reduce the heat and simmer until the lettuce is wilted, but still a little crunchy, about 5 minutes.

3 When the pasta is done, drain it and add it to the skillet. Add the mint, parsley, and remaining 2 tablespoons butter. Bring to a rapid simmer over high heat and reduce the sauce until it coats the pasta with a shiny glaze, 1 to 2 minutes, adding a little more chicken stock if the pan seems dry. Remove the skillet from the heat, sprinkle with the cheese, toss, and serve.

38 STOCK
VEGETABLE

As with chicken stock, the ideal scenario would be to save your vegetable scraps and make your own, but when this is not possible, there are good-quality vegetable stocks available at the grocery store. I prefer the cartons over the cans for flavor and cost.

The quality, color, and clarity of vegetable stock will vary greatly depending on the brand and the vegetables used. Some are more brothy and clear, some are darker and thicker, almost like a thin soup. The brothier varieties are better as a general ingredient as they are more neutral in flavor.

Tips

■ Purchase low-sodium stock, and in cartons, if available.

■ Vegetable stock keeps in the pantry for a year or more. (Check the expiration date.) Once opened, keep sealed and refrigerated and it will keep for 3 or 4 more days.

FRESH HERB TEA SOUP

This soup is light and restorative but with a deep savory flavor from the vegetable stock and tea. It's perfect to make the day after a heavy meal or night out or when you are getting over a cold. ▪ **SERVES 4 TO 6**

6 cups vegetable stock

2 green tea bags

2 cups thinly sliced button mushrooms

1 cup julienned canned bamboo shoots

1 cup coconut milk

1 teaspoon hot chile sauce, such as Sriracha

2 tablespoons chopped fresh basil

2 tablespoons chopped fresh chervil

2 tablespoons chopped fresh Italian parsley

2 tablespoons chopped fresh tarragon

Juice of 1 to 2 limes or lemons

Kosher salt

1 Pour the stock in a medium saucepan and add the tea bags. Bring just to a simmer, remove from the heat, and let steep for 3 minutes. Discard the tea bags.

2 Return to a simmer and add the mushrooms, bamboo shoots, coconut milk, and chile sauce. Return to a simmer and cook until the mushrooms are tender, about 10 minutes. Add the basil, chervil, parsley, and tarragon. Remove from the heat and let steep for 10 minutes to infuse the soup with the flavors of the herbs.

3 Return the soup to a simmer and then stir in the lime juice and salt to taste. Serve hot.

LITTLE GEM LETTUCE SOUP
WITH CRÈME FRAÎCHE

VEGETABLE
GAZPACHO

FRESH HERB
TEA SOUP

LITTLE GEM LETTUCE SOUP
WITH CRÈME FRAÎCHE

I like to use a light vegetable stock here so the soup stays a deep green after pureeing, and the stock does not overpower the sweetness of the lettuce. The ham hock adds a pleasant savory touch but can easily be omitted for a vegetarian soup. ■ SERVES 4

3 tablespoons extra-virgin olive oil

1 medium onion, diced (about 1 cup)

1 garlic clove, crushed

1 quart vegetable stock

1 small ham hock, rinsed well (optional)

1 cup frozen peas, thawed

4 heads Little Gem lettuce, cored, washed, and chopped

½ cup fresh Italian parsley leaves

1 small avocado, pitted, peeled, and diced

½ cup crème fraîche

Juice of 2 limes (about ¼ cup)

Kosher salt and freshly ground black pepper

1 In a medium saucepan, heat the oil over medium heat. Add the onion and garlic and cook until the onion is tender, about 10 minutes.

2 Add the vegetable stock, 1 cup water, and ham hock (if using). Bring to a simmer and cook to combine flavors, about 10 minutes.

3 Add the peas and lettuce and simmer until very tender, 10 to 12 minutes, adding the parsley in the last 2 minutes of cooking.

4 Remove the ham hock and transfer the soup to a blender. Shred the meat from the ham hock and set aside. Add the avocado, ¼ cup of the crème fraîche, and 1 tablespoon of the lime juice to the blender. Puree until smooth (be careful blending hot liquids!). Return to the saucepan along with the shredded ham to rewarm and season with salt and pepper.

5 To serve, in a small bowl stir together the remaining ¼ cup crème fraîche and the remaining lime juice. Serve the soup in bowls, with the lime crème fraîche drizzled over.

VEGETABLE GAZPACHO

Vegetable stock has a saline savoriness that I love. Instead of adding water to thin the gazpacho, as some other recipes do, I add vegetable stock to reinforce the flavors of the fresh vegetables. ■ **SERVES 4**

2 cups cored, seeded, and diced ripe tomato (about 3 medium tomatoes)

1 cup seeded and diced Kirby cucumber (about 1 large Kirby)

1 cup chopped yellow or red bell pepper

½ cup halved seedless green grapes

½ cup fresh Italian parsley leaves

¼ cup diced red onion

1 small garlic clove, smashed

¼ cup red wine vinegar

½ teaspoon ground cumin

¼ cup extra-virgin olive oil

½ cup vegetable stock, plus more as needed

Kosher salt and freshly ground black pepper

1 In a blender, combine the tomato, cucumber, bell pepper, grapes, parsley, onion, garlic, vinegar, and cumin. Puree until almost smooth. With the blender running, pour in the oil in a slow steady stream until the gazpacho is smooth.

2 Add ½ cup of the vegetable stock and blend again. If the gazpacho is too thick for you, add more stock, until you achieve a consistency that you like. Season with salt and pepper and chill in a pitcher or bowl before serving.

SUGAR
CONFECTIONERS'

39

Confectioners' sugar (also called powdered sugar) is white sugar in a powdered form with about 3 percent cornstarch added to prevent clumping. Because of the added cornstarch, it should not be substituted for granulated, brown, or any other kind of sugar.

This sugar is most commonly used in frosting, whipped cream, sauces, and candies where the sugar needs to dissolve without heating. I love confectioners' sugar because of its versatility, and I feel prepared knowing I can make fresh whipped cream at a moment's notice. Buy a tart and make your own whipped cream, which adds a "homemade" effect for your guests.

Tips

- Always sift confectioners' sugar before using, even if the recipe doesn't specify it, to remove lumps.

- Confectioners' sugar will keep indefinitely in the pantry. Store in an airtight container and keep away from moisture.

- A dusting of confectioners' sugar is a simple last-minute garnish for chocolate and fruit desserts . . . or my favorite, soufflés!

WHISKEY SAUCE

CINNAMON
CUPCAKES
WITH VANILLA
FROSTING

CLASSIC
WHIPPED
CREAM

CLASSIC WHIPPED CREAM

To achieve the maximum airiness and height with whipped cream, make sure the cream is very cold and chill the work bowl and whisk attachment in the freezer before using. Confectioners' sugar is best in whipped cream because it dissolves immediately, unlike granulated sugar, which stays gritty. ■ **SERVES 6**

1½ cups very cold heavy cream
½ vanilla bean, split lengthwise

3 tablespoons confectioners' sugar, sifted

1 In the chilled bowl of an electric mixer, add the cream. With the tip of a paring knife, scrape in the seeds from the vanilla bean. With the whisk attachment, mix on medium speed until the cream begins to hold very soft peaks, 1 to 2 minutes.

2 Add the confectioners' sugar and whisk on high speed to soft peaks, just 1 minute longer. Use immediately or chill for a few hours, rewhipping with a whisk before serving.

CINNAMON CUPCAKES
WITH VANILLA FROSTING

This classic frosting is as easy and foolproof as it gets, and these cupcakes are best served within an hour or two after frosting. If you must refrigerate, let them sit at room temperature again for thirty minutes or so before serving. ▪ **MAKES 1 DOZEN CUPCAKES**

CUPCAKES

1½ cups all-purpose flour

1½ teaspoons baking powder

1¼ teaspoons ground cinnamon

¼ teaspoon kosher salt

¼ pound (1 stick) unsalted butter, at room temperature

1 cup granulated sugar

2 large eggs, at room temperature

1 teaspoon pure vanilla extract

1 cup whole milk

VANILLA FROSTING

½ pound (2 sticks) unsalted butter, at room temperature

3 cups confectioners' sugar, sifted

½ teaspoon pure vanilla extract

Ground cinnamon, for garnish (optional)

1 To make the cupcakes: Preheat the oven to 350°F. Line a 12-cup cupcake tin with paper liners.

2 Sift together the flour, baking powder, cinnamon, and salt.

3 In the bowl of an electric mixer fitted with the paddle attachment, beat the butter and granulated sugar on medium high until light and fluffy, about 2 minutes. Add the eggs, one at a time, beating until incorporated after adding each egg. Scrape down the sides of the work bowl and beat in the vanilla.

4 On low speed, add the flour mixture in 3 additions, alternating with the milk, beginning and ending with the dry ingredients. Raise the speed to medium high and beat just until the batter is smooth, about 10 seconds.

5 Divide the batter among the paper liners and bake until a tester inserted in a cupcake comes out clean, about 20 minutes. Remove the cupcakes from the tin and cool completely on a cooling rack.

6 To make the frosting: In a clean mixer bowl, beat the butter on medium high until pale yellow and smooth, about 2 minutes. Add the confectioners' sugar ½ cup at a time, mixing on low to incorporate and then increasing the speed to high for 15 seconds with each addition to aerate the frosting. Once all the sugar has been added, scrape down the sides of the bowl, add the vanilla, and beat on high 1 minute, until very light, fluffy, and smooth.

7 The frosting can be smoothed on the cooled cupcakes with an offset spatula or piped from a pastry bag fitted with a large star tip. (If making these cupcakes on a very warm day, put the frosting back in the refrigerator for 10 minutes before trying to pipe.) Sprinkle with ground cinnamon, if desired, and serve.

WHISKEY SAUCE

This sauce is the perfect topping for vanilla ice cream or a chunk of warm bread pudding. You can make this ahead and reheat gently in the microwave on short time bursts or in a double boiler. ■ **MAKES ABOUT I CUP**

I cup confectioners' sugar, sifted

¾ cup heavy cream, warmed

¼ cup bourbon, preferably Elijah Craig

I In a medium saucepan over medium-low heat, add the confectioners' sugar. Cook, without moving the pot, until the sugar begins to melt, about 3 minutes. Continue to cook,whisking occasionally to break up any lumps, until the sugar is completely melted and golden brown, 3 to 4 minutes.

2 Pour in the warm cream. The mixture may solidify. Raise the heat to medium and simmer, stirring, until the mixture melts again and is smooth, about 3 minutes. Take the pot off the heat and carefully add the bourbon. Return to the heat, bring to a boil, and simmer 1 minute to cook off some of the harshness of the bourbon. Let cool at least 10 minutes before serving, but serve warm.

SUGAR
GRANULATED

40

Granulated sugar, made from sugarcane, is the most common type of sugar. It has a sandy texture and simple, sweet flavor that makes it the go-to sweetener for baking and drinks. When it is ground, it becomes superfine sugar or confectioners' sugar (with added cornstarch). Coarse or sanding sugar is the same product processed in a coarser grind.

Granulated sugar will keep indefinitely in the pantry, though you will likely use it so often you won't have to worry about that.

Tips

- Make sure your sugar container is tightly sealed to keep out moisture and other odors or flavors.

- Always measure sugar by spooning into a dry measuring cup and leveling with the back of a knife.

DARK AND STORMY
WITH GINGERED
SIMPLE SYRUP

QUICK CARAMELIZED
APPLE TART

CRANBERRY
RELISH

DARK AND STORMY
WITH GINGERED SIMPLE SYRUP

Basic simple syrup is just equal parts sugar and water, cooked until the sugar dissolves and then chilled. You can use this to sweeten myriad cold drinks, iced tea, iced coffee, and, of course, cocktails. I add ginger and lime to the syrup here to highlight the flavors of this classic cocktail. ■ **SERVES 4**

½ cup sugar

2 tablespoons grated peeled fresh ginger

Zest of 1 lime, removed with a vegetable peeler

Juice of 1 lime (about 2 tablespoons juice)

8 ounces dark rum

2 12-ounce cans ginger beer, preferably Gosling's

1 lime, cut into wedges, for garnish

Mint sprigs, for garnish

1 Chill 4 highball glasses in the freezer. In a small saucepan, combine ½ cup water, the sugar, ginger, and lime zest strips. Bring to a simmer and cook just until the sugar is dissolved. Let steep 30 minutes and then strain. Stir the lime juice into the syrup.

2 Remove the glasses from the freezer and fill with ice cubes. Divide the syrup and rum among the glasses. Fill to the top with ginger beer. Stir and garnish with the lime wedges and the mint.

QUICK CARAMELIZED APPLE TART

This is my quick version of tarte tatin, a classic and infinitely chic French dessert. The sugar and butter melt together to make a simple caramel sauce that coats the tart once it is inverted, so no extra sauce or garnish is needed.

■ SERVES 8

All-purpose flour, for rolling the pastry

1 sheet frozen puff pastry, thawed in the refrigerator

2 tablespoons (¼ stick) unsalted butter

½ cup sugar

4 medium Golden Delicious apples, peeled, cored, and cut into eighths

1 Preheat the oven to 425°F. On a floured work surface, roll the puff pastry into a 12-inch square, about ⅛ inch thick. Invert a 10-inch ovenproof nonstick skillet over the pastry. Using the skillet as a guide, cut a 10-inch round of pastry. Transfer to a plate and chill in the refrigerator while you prepare the apples.

2 Heat the same skillet over medium heat. Melt the butter and then sprinkle over the sugar and add the apples on top. Once the sugar begins to melt, adjust the heat so the juices bubble rapidly. Cook, stirring, until the apples are tender and juices are light golden brown, 10 to 12 minutes. Remove from the heat.

3 Using a fork, nudge the apples into 2 concentric circles (it doesn't have to be perfect) in the skillet. Top with the chilled pastry round and tuck the edges in. Gently prick the pastry in 4 or 5 places with a fork. Bake for 10 minutes at 425°F., until the pastry is puffed and light golden. Reduce the oven temperature to 375°F. and bake until the pastry is a deep golden brown, 10 to 12 minutes more. Remove from the oven and let sit 10 minutes.

4 To unmold, place a serving plate over the skillet and quickly but carefully flip the pan. The tart will unmold onto the plate, and if a few apples slices stick to the pan, return them to the tart. Let cool at least 20 minutes before serving to allow the syrup to sink into the tart. Serve slightly warm or at room temperature.

CRANBERRY RELISH

This relish can be made two or three days ahead, making it easy to check one thing off the list for a holiday meal. Any leftovers can be spread on a sandwich or folded into a simple muffin recipe. ■ **MAKES 2 CUPS**

1 12-ounce bag fresh cranberries, rinsed and picked over

1 cup sugar

Finely grated zest and juice of 1 lemon (about 3 tablespoons juice)

Finely grated zest and juice of 1 lime (about 2 tablespoons juice)

Kosher salt and freshly ground black pepper

1 In a medium saucepan over medium heat, combine the cranberries, sugar, lemon zest and juice, lime zest and juice, and ¼ cup water. Bring to a rapid simmer and cook until the berries begin to pop, about 2 minutes. Reduce the heat so the mixture is just barely simmering and cook until thick, about 5 minutes.

2 Remove from the heat and season with salt and pepper. Cool and serve either chilled or at room temperature.

41 SUGAR
LIGHT BROWN

Brown sugar is granulated sugar with molasses added for enhanced flavor and texture. Light brown sugar simply has less molasses added than dark brown, so they can be interchanged, though dark brown has a slightly richer flavor. Brown sugar can generally be substituted for granulated sugar in recipes, though the final product will be darker and moister.

Store brown sugar in a sealed airtight plastic bag in the pantry. Eventually, brown sugar will harden. If this happens, sometimes you can revive it for one more use by putting the hardened sugar in a covered bowl in the microwave and sticking a damp paper towel in the back of the microwave. Set for 20 to 25 seconds or until the sugar softens enough to measure.

Tips

- In a pinch, brown sugar can be made by stirring 1 or 2 tablespoons of molasses into 1 cup of granulated sugar.

- I like to add a couple tablespoons of brown sugar to dry rubs for meat and poultry to help caramelize the surface of the meat when grilling or roasting.

BROWN SUGAR AND BLACK PEPPER BACON

You can make this with regular thin-sliced grocery store bacon, though I prefer the thick-sliced applewood-smoked variety. If using thin-sliced bacon, start checking it for doneness after about fifteen minutes. Maple adds great flavor to the bacon, but the brown sugar is what helps it stick and caramelize. These make for a delicious canapé and are best served upright in a tall glass, like breadsticks. ■ SERVES 4 TO 6

¼ cup (packed) light brown sugar

¼ cup pure maple syrup

1 teaspoon coarsely ground black pepper

Finely grated zest of 2 limes

12 thick slices applewood-smoked bacon

1 Preheat the oven to 350°F. In a small bowl, stir together the sugar, syrup, pepper, and lime zest.

2 Put the bacon on a rack on a rimmed sheet pan lined with foil for easier cleanup. Brush with the sugar mixture, flip, and brush the other side.

3 Bake until the fat is rendered, the bacon is crisp, and the glaze is bubbly, about 20 minutes. Let cool on the rack for 5 minutes before serving. Do not drain on paper towels; the bacon will stick.

MIXED BERRY CRUMBLE

Brown sugar is an essential ingredient in a crumble to achieve those crisp, caramelized bits on top that we all love. I like to serve individual crumbles, but if you don't have six ramekins, this can also be made in a medium-size oval baking dish. Make sure to bake the crumble on a rimmed sheet pan lined with foil to catch any drips. ▪ SERVES 6

4 cups mixed fresh berries, such as any combination of blueberries, raspberries, and blackberries

½ cup granulated sugar

2 tablespoons cornstarch

Finely grated zest and juice of 1 lemon (about 3 tablespoons juice)

½ cup all-purpose flour

½ cup (packed) light brown sugar

½ teaspoon ground cinnamon

Pinch of kosher salt

½ cup rolled oats (not instant)

6 tablespoons (¾ stick) cold unsalted butter, cut into pieces

Classic Whipped Cream (page 233) or crème fraîche, for serving

1 Preheat the oven to 350°F. In a medium bowl, toss the berries with the granulated sugar, cornstarch, and lemon zest and juice. Let sit at room temperature 15 minutes, stirring occasionally.

2 For the topping, in a food processor, add the flour, brown sugar, cinnamon, and salt and pulse to combine. Add the oats and sprinkle the butter pieces on top. Pulse in quick bursts just until the butter is distributed and the size of small peas.

3 Divide the berries among six 6-ounce ramekins on a rimmed sheet pan lined with foil. Sprinkle the topping evenly over all of the ramekins; do not pack down. It may seem like a lot of topping, but use it all, as it sinks into the crumbles as they bake.

4 Bake until the topping is crisp and brown and the berries are bubbling, about 35 minutes. Let cool 10 minutes before serving, but the crumbles are best served warm, with a dollop of whipped cream.

BROWN SUGAR AND
BLACK PEPPER BACON

BROWN
SUGAR PIE

MIXED BERRY
CRUMBLE

BROWN SUGAR PIE

This old-fashioned pie tastes like pecan pie without the pecans. It's very sweet and rich, so a small slice goes a long way. It is best served still slightly warm or at room temperature but never chilled. It's also one of the easiest pies you can make—just mix and pour into a pie shell—which makes it a great recipe for beginning pie makers. I like to eat it with a dollop of crème fraîche to cut the sweetness. ■ SERVES 8 TO 10

2 large eggs, at room temperature

2 cups (lightly packed) light brown sugar

⅓ cup half-and-half

4 tablespoons (½ stick) unsalted butter, melted and cooled

2 teaspoons pure vanilla extract

⅓ cup all-purpose flour

1 8- or 9-inch unbaked pie shell

Crème fraîche, for serving

1 Preheat the oven to 350°F. In the bowl of an electric mixer fitted with the paddle attachment, combine the eggs, sugar, and half-and-half. Beat on medium speed until smooth, about 1 minute. Add the melted butter and vanilla and mix to combine. Sprinkle the flour over the top and mix just until smooth and no lumps remain.

2 Pour the filling into the pie shell and bake in the middle of the oven until the pie is just set and no longer wobbly in the center, about 40 minutes. (If the crust is getting too brown and the pie is still not set, cover the edges of the crust with foil.) Let cool on a wire rack. Serve slightly warm or at room temperature. When plating, top each slice with a dollop of crème fraîche.

Earl Grey is a blend of black tea leaves with the addition of bergamot oil, which gives it a distinctive perfume. It is one of the most popular teas available in the Western world and is enjoyed for its bright and bold citrusy taste. At home, I prefer the ease of individually packaged bags to preserve freshness, but loose tea stored in tins is beautiful. For loose tea, you need a strainer or disposable muslin or paper bag to prevent "swimming" leaves in your hot water. If brewing loose tea, I teaspoon equals I tea bag for the recipes here.

Because of its citrus flavor, Earl Grey is often used in pastry and baking. When brewing tea to drink, use I bag per cup of water. For cooking, add an extra bag or two, depending on how forward you want the tea flavor to be, to concentrate the tea flavor so the other ingredients do not overpower it.

Tips

- The caffeine in tea, although less than coffee overall, has a more sustained impact than the caffeine in coffee. Where a cup of coffee gives a quick spike of caffeine, a cup of tea allows for a gradual build in your body and the effect of the caffeine lasts for a much longer time.

- When buying tea bags, look for a brand that uses muslin or some sort of loose material. A loose bag allows for the leaves to expand as they unfurl in the water, and the bag is stitched with thread so you are not steeping glue or staples, found on more mainstream bags, in your tea.

- It is worth spending money on quality tea. Many cheap teas most likely have tea dust in the bags, not true quality leaves. They are also known to have dyes to color your drink (or food) quickly, giving it the effect of "working."

EARL GREY ICED TEA
WITH ICED TEA CUBES

Earl Grey makes a particularly refreshing and almost sophisticated iced tea, but you can make this with any tea you choose, or follow the same basic method and make iced coffee with iced coffee cubes. This recipe is easily doubled or tripled—just make sure you have enough ice-cube trays!

■ **SERVES 2**

5 Earl Grey tea bags

3 to 4 tablespoons superfine sugar

Fresh mint sprigs, for garnish

1 Place 2 glasses in the freezer. In a medium saucepan, bring 2½ cups cold water to a boil. Remove from the heat, add the tea bags, and let steep 5 minutes. Discard the tea bags. Stir in the sugar, to taste. Add 1 cup cold water.

2 Pour about half the tea into ice-cube trays and freeze. Chill the remaining tea in the refrigerator.

3 When ready to serve, place the ice cubes in the chilled glasses, pour the tea over, and garnish with mint.

FRENCH TOAST WITH EARL GREY SYRUP

When I created this special syrup, I had been trying to come up with an interesting and unique brunch condiment. I then simply steeped Earl Grey tea in a one-to-one sugar and water solution, and the end result tasted fantastic paired with French toast. This easy syrup can be made ahead and rewarmed in a small saucepan or in the microwave when ready to serve. Any leftover syrup can be used to sweeten hot tea or stored in the refrigerator for later use. ■ SERVES 4

EARL GREY SYRUP

1 cup sugar

4 Earl Grey tea bags

FRENCH TOAST

4 large eggs

¾ cup whole milk

¾ cup heavy cream

2 tablespoons sugar

1 teaspoon pure vanilla extract

Pinch of kosher salt

2 tablespoons (¼ stick) unsalted butter, plus more for serving

8 1-inch-thick slices challah bread or good-quality white bread

1 To make the syrup: In a small saucepan, bring 1 cup water to a boil. Add the sugar and simmer until the sugar is dissolved. Remove from the heat, add the tea bags, and let steep 5 minutes. Discard the teas bags. Bring the sweetened tea to a rapid simmer and cook until syrupy (about the thickness of real maple syrup), 6 to 7 minutes. You should have about ¾ cup syrup.

2 To make the French toast: Preheat the oven to 250°F. In a large bowl, whisk together the eggs, milk, cream, sugar, vanilla, and salt. In a large nonstick skillet, melt 1 tablespoon of the butter over medium heat. Submerge 4 slices of the bread in the egg mixture and let soak about 30 seconds, turning to make sure the slices are evenly soaked. Let the excess egg mixture drip back into the bowl.

3 Cook the bread in the butter until golden on both sides, 2 to 3 minutes per side. Keep the first batch warm in the oven while you make the second batch with the remaining 1 tablespoon butter and the last 4 slices of bread. Serve the French toast warm with additional butter and drizzle with the warm Earl Grey syrup.

FRENCH
TOAST WITH
EARL GREY
SYRUP

EARL GREY ICED TEA WITH ICED TEA CUBES

BOMBOLONI WITH EARL GREY CREAM

BOMBOLONI WITH EARL GREY CREAM

I was introduced to bomboloni, basically an Italian doughnut, in the early 1980s when I was working in the pastry department at Le Cirque in New York. Of course, I fell in love with these doughy pillows. For my take on them, the addition of Earl Grey to the pastry cream rounds it out and keeps the bomboloni from being cloyingly sweet. Be sure to start the dough a day ahead and take care not to overfill the bomboloni, or they can burst.

■ MAKES ABOUT 4 DOZEN BOMBOLONI

BOMBOLONI

2 packages (4½ teaspoons) active dry yeast

¼ cup warm water (90 to 100°F., just warm to the touch)

3½ cups all-purpose flour, plus more as needed

1⅓ cups plus a pinch of sugar

4 large eggs, at room temperature

½ teaspoon kosher salt

1 stick plus 6 tablespoons cold unsalted butter, cut into pieces

Canola oil, for oiling the bowl and frying

Cooking spray

EARL GREY CREAM

2 cups whole milk

4 Earl Grey tea bags

5 large egg yolks

½ cup sugar

¼ cup cornstarch

Pinch of kosher salt

1 teaspoon pure vanilla extract

1 To make the bomboloni: In a spouted measuring cup, stir together the yeast, water, and a pinch of sugar. Let proof until bubbly, about 5 minutes.

2 In the bowl of an electric mixer fitted with the paddle attachment, combine the flour, ⅓ cup of the sugar, eggs, and salt and mix on medium speed until just combined. Increase the speed to medium high and add the butter a few pieces at a time until all is incorporated. Mix on high for 1 minute. The dough should come together in a mass but still be a little sticky; it should not completely clean the sides of the bowl. If the dough is still too wet, add up to ¼ cup more flour, a few tablespoons at a time, until the dough comes together in a mass. Gather the dough into a ball and transfer to an oiled bowl and let rest at room temperature for 30 minutes and then cover with plastic wrap and refrigerate overnight. (The dough will not rise very much in the refrigerator.)

3 To make the Earl Grey cream: In a medium saucepan, bring the milk to a bare simmer. Remove from the heat, add the tea bags, and let steep 3 minutes. Discard the tea bags. In a large bowl, whisk together the egg yolks, sugar, cornstarch, and salt until smooth. Whisk in the milk in a slow, steady stream, whisking constantly so the yolks don't scramble. When all of the milk has been mixed in, pour everything back into the saucepan and cook, stirring, over low heat until the mixture has thickened and a few bubbles appear at the surface. Strain the mixture into a clean bowl, stir in the vanilla, and cover the surface of the pastry cream with a piece of plastic wrap or parchment paper. Refrigerate until chilled, at least 4 hours or overnight.

4 After the dough has proofed overnight, remove from the refrigerator and, on a floured work surface, roll or press the dough to about ½ inch thick. Using a 1½-inch-round cutter, cut out as many rounds as you can. You should get about 4 dozen. Line 2 baking sheets with plastic wrap and spray with cooking spray. Arrange the bomboloni on the baking sheets, not touching. Cover loosely with another sheet of plastic wrap sprayed with cooking spray. Let rise until doubled, about 1½ hours.

5 When you are ready to fry the bomboloni, heat about 2 inches of oil in a deep straight-sided skillet to 350°F. Fill a pastry bag fitted with a medium plain tip with the pastry cream. Spread the remaining 1 cup sugar in a shallow bowl and line a sheet pan with paper towels.

6 Fry the bomboloni in several batches, about 2 minutes per side. (They will puff substantially, so don't put too many in the skillet at once.) Drain on paper towels. Once you have fried them all, roll the hot bomboloni in the sugar. With a paring knife, make a hole in the top of each bomboloni just large enough to fit the pastry tip. Stick the tip in the center of the bomboloni, gently squeeze the bag, and add some of the filling to each bomboloni. These are best served right after filling but can be made a few hours ahead and refrigerated.

43 TABASCO
RED

Tabasco hot pepper sauce was created by Edward McIlhenny on Avery Island in Louisiana in 1868 and has been in the family ever since. The peppers are still grown on Avery Island (and some in Latin America, since the demand is so high). After the peppers are picked, they are mashed with salt and fermented in barrels for up to 3 years. The peppers are then mixed with distilled vinegar, strained, and bottled.

The hot sauce should not light your tongue on fire at first taste or it will render any seasonings and flavors imperceptible. Red Tabasco is the benchmark against which I measure all other hot sauces because it has just the right balance of spice and acidity. And a little goes a long way. The green (jalapeño) version of the sauce is slightly milder, for when you want an even gentler hit of heat.

Tips

- Tabasco can be stored, tightly sealed, in the pantry and keeps almost indefinitely.

- Tabasco may separate if it is not used for a long period of time. Simply shake to reemulsify and use.

BEEF TARTARE WITH CRISPY POTATOES AND TABASCO-BONITO DRESSING

Since it's hard to split an egg yolk for the dressing, this makes a little more than you need. The dressing is basically a spicy mayo, so use any extra as a sandwich spread or to dress cooked potatoes or vegetables. Bonito flakes are dried, fermented, and smoked skipjack tuna that is then shaved into flakes that are a staple Japanese seasoning. You can find them at Asian food stores or online. ■ SERVES 6

I large organic egg yolk

2 tablespoons capers, drained

I tablespoon red Tabasco sauce

I tablespoon white wine vinegar

I teaspoon Dijon mustard

I teaspoon bonito flakes

¼ cup canola oil, plus more for frying the potatoes

¼ cup extra-virgin olive oil

Kosher salt and freshly ground black pepper

4 fingerling potatoes

12 ounces beef tenderloin, trimmed of all fat and very finely diced

2 tablespoons finely minced shallots

Finely grated zest of I small lemon

2 tablespoons chopped fresh chives

1 In a blender or mini food processor, combine the egg yolk, capers, Tabasco, vinegar, mustard, and bonito flakes. Blend to combine. With the machine running, add ¼ cup of the canola oil and the olive oil in a slow, steady stream to make a thick dressing. Season with salt and pepper and chill until thick, about 1 hour.

2 Meanwhile, heat 2 inches of canola oil to 350°F. in a medium saucepan. Very thinly slice the potatoes lengthwise on a mandoline (if you have one) or by hand. Fry the potato slices in 2 batches until golden brown and crisp, 1 to 2 minutes per batch. Drain on paper towels and season with salt while still hot.

3 When ready to serve, toss the beef with the shallots and lemon zest. Toss with enough dressing to coat well. Divide the beef onto serving plates with the potatoes and sprinkle with chives.

BEEF TARTARE
WITH CRISPY POTATOES
AND TABASCO-BONITO
DRESSING

• MINI GRUYÈRE
AND BLACK OLIVE
PANINI WITH
HOT SAUCE

THREE-MEAT CHILI

THREE-MEAT CHILI

This is a simple, spicy meat chili with a good deal of the heat coming from both red and green Tabasco. If you like, you can add vegetables or beans, but I don't think it needs it—though I do like to add a cool dollop of crème fraîche. For really stellar chili, buy your meat whole and grind it yourself or ask your butcher to coarsely grind it on the spot for you. ■ **SERVES A CROWD, 8 OR MORE**

3 tablespoons extra-virgin olive oil

1 pound ground beef chuck

1 pound ground pork shoulder

1 pound ground veal shoulder

Kosher salt and freshly ground black pepper

2 large onions, chopped (about 3 cups)

6 garlic cloves, finely chopped

2 bunches scallions (white and green parts), chopped (about 2 cups)

2 tablespoons tomato paste

6 tablespoons chili powder

1 12-ounce bottle dark beer, such as Dos Equis

2 28-ounce cans fire-roasted tomatoes with juice, crushed by hand

2 cups chicken stock

2 tablespoons red Tabasco sauce

2 tablespoons green Tabasco sauce

1 cup crème fraîche, lightly whipped and chilled, for serving

1 In a large Dutch oven, heat the oil over medium-high heat. When the oil is hot, add the beef, pork, and veal. Cook and stir occasionally until the meats are browned all over and you can hear a slight crackling in the pot, letting you know the moisture has cooked away, about 15 minutes. Season with salt and pepper.

2 Reduce the heat to medium. Add the onions, garlic, and scallions and cook until wilted, about 5 minutes. Make a space in the pan and drop in the tomato paste. Let toast for 1 minute and then stir into the meat. Sprinkle in the chili powder. Cook and stir until fragrant, about 2 minutes.

3 Pour in the beer and cook until almost reduced away, about 4 minutes. Pour in the tomatoes and stock and season with the red and green Tabasco. Adjust the heat so the chili is gently simmering and cook, uncovered, until the chili is thick, dark red, and flavorful, about 1½ hours. Serve in bowls with a dollop of crème fraîche.

MINI GRUYÈRE AND BLACK OLIVE PANINI WITH HOT SAUCE

These panini can be served as finger food at a casual party or with tomato soup for a heart- and soul-warming lunch. ■ SERVES 4

2 tablespoons (¼ stick) unsalted butter, melted

4 teaspoons red Tabasco sauce, plus more for serving

½ cup pitted brine-cured black olives, such as Kalamata

2 tablespoons capers, drained

2 tablespoons chopped fresh Italian parsley

1 small garlic clove, chopped

1 anchovy fillet, chopped

2 tablespoons extra-virgin olive oil

8 ½-inch-thick slices country bread from a long oval loaf

½ cup sliced roasted marinated red peppers, patted dry

6 ounces thinly sliced Gruyère cheese

1 In a small bowl, whisk together the melted butter and 2 teaspoons of the Tabasco.

2 In a mini food processor, combine the olives, capers, parsley, garlic, and anchovy and pulse to make a chunky paste. With the machine running, drizzle in the oil and remaining 2 teaspoons Tabasco to make an almost smooth paste. Scrape into a bowl.

3 Spread the paste on 4 slices of bread. Top with the peppers, then the cheese, and another slice of bread, pressing down to compress the sandwiches.

4 Heat a cast-iron skillet over medium heat. (Ideally, make all of the panini in 1 batch, but if your skillet isn't large enough, make them in 2 batches, saving some of the butter for the second batch.) Pour in half the butter-Tabasco mixture and swirl in the skillet and then add the panini. Cover with another skillet and press down to flatten. Leave the skillet on, pressing occasionally, and cook until the panini are toasted on 1 side, about 3 minutes. Flip and add the remaining butter–Tabasco mixture, moving the panini around so the bottoms get coated in the butter. Repeat the pressing and toasting until golden on the second side and the cheese is melted, about 3 minutes. Remove to a cutting board and let sit 2 minutes. With a serrated knife, cut each sandwich crosswise into 4 sticks or in halves. Serve immediately with a bottle of hot sauce for garnish.

TOMATOES
CANNED

Canned tomatoes are amazingly effective, extremely underrated, and invaluable in the pantry. They should always be kept on hand. Always purchase canned tomatoes that are whole, peeled, and in their juice. Even if a recipe calls for crushed tomatoes or tomato puree, still buy the whole canned tomatoes and do it yourself, because companies use the highest-quality tomatoes for canning whole.

In the height of summer when farm-fresh tomatoes are at their peak, I try to use them as much as possible. The rest of the year, canned tomatoes are an extremely worthy substitute. I never can tomatoes myself as there are so many wonderful ones to buy. I prefer brands that use San Marzano tomatoes, a variety of plum tomatoes with thick flesh that has the perfect balance of sweet and acid and, as a result, produces a superior sauce. True San Marzanos come from the Valle del Sarno in Italy and will have a DOP seal. Always make sure your pantry shelves have at least one can.

Tips

- One can of tomatoes with 2 tablespoons oil put through a food mill makes a quick, easy pizza sauce.

- Do not put tomatoes directly from the can into a blender or food processor; it will aerate them too much and make them pink, not the deep red you want from canned tomatoes. Instead, dump a can of whole tomatoes in a bowl and crush by hand or put through a food mill to get the texture and color you want.

SUMMER TOMATO SOUP WITH CUCUMBER-DILL YOGURT

QUICK TOMATO SAUCE

BRAISED GREEN BEANS WITH TOMATOES

QUICK TOMATO SAUCE

This is a great basic tomato sauce. Just finish with $^1/_2$ cup of grated Parmigiano-Reggiano when tossing with the pasta. It also takes well to additions—a handful of capers, olives, crisped pancetta, or even a can of drained tuna. ■ MAKES ABOUT 2½ CUPS, ENOUGH TO SAUCE 1 POUND PASTA

¼ cup extra-virgin olive oil

1 cup finely chopped onion

1 28-ounce can whole plum tomatoes with juice

4 garlic cloves, sliced

Pinch of crushed red pepper flakes

½ teaspoon dried oregano

Kosher salt

¼ cup fresh basil leaves

1 In a large skillet, heat the oil over medium heat. When the oil is hot, add the onion. Cook, stirring occasionally, until the onion is softened, about 8 minutes.

2 Meanwhile, pour the tomatoes and their juice in a medium bowl. Crush the tomatoes with your hands, leaving a little texture.

3 When the onion has softened, raise the heat to medium high and add the garlic and pepper flakes. Cook and stir until the garlic is sizzling and fragrant, about 1 minute. Add the tomatoes, fill the tomato can with about 1¼ cups water, and add that to the skillet as well. Stir in the oregano and season with salt. Bring to a simmer and cook until thickened, about 15 minutes. Coarsely tear the basil leaves and stir into the sauce just before serving.

BRAISED GREEN BEANS WITH TOMATOES

Green beans are usually served crisp-tender, but in this recipe they are best cooked to the point of falling apart. They soak up all the flavors of this spiced tomato sauce and are a great side to pork, lamb, or chicken.

■ **SERVES 4 TO 6**

3 tablespoons extra-virgin olive oil

1 medium onion, thickly sliced

2 banana peppers, seeded and sliced

1 28-ounce can whole plum tomatoes with juice

3 garlic cloves, sliced

1 teaspoon ground cumin

1 teaspoon smoked paprika

¼ teaspoon ground cinnamon

1 pound green beans, trimmed

2 dried bay leaves

½ cup pitted and halved Kalamata olives

¼ cup coarsely chopped fresh basil

1 In a Dutch oven, heat the oil over medium heat. Add the onion and peppers and cook until wilted, about 10 minutes. Meanwhile, pour the tomatoes and their juice in a medium bowl. Crush the tomatoes with your hands, leaving a little texture.

2 Once the vegetables are wilted, add the garlic, cumin, paprika, and cinnamon and cook until fragrant, about 1 minute. Add the green beans and bay leaves and toss to coat in the oil. Raise the heat to medium high and add the tomatoes. Fill the tomato can with ½ cup water and add to the sauce. Bring to a simmer, cover, and cook for 15 minutes.

3 Uncover, stir in the olives and basil, cover again, and cook until the sauce is thick and beans tender, about 15 minutes more. Remove the bay leaves and serve hot.

SUMMER TOMATO SOUP
WITH CUCUMBER-DILL YOGURT

This soup is light and refreshing when chilled, but it is also great served hot in the wintertime. The tangy yogurt dolloped on top is the perfect counterbalance for the slight sweetness of this soup. ■ **SERVES 4**

SOUP

3 tablespoons extra-virgin olive oil

I small onion, finely chopped (about I cup)

½ cup grated carrot

I teaspoon grated orange zest

Juice of I small orange (about ¼ cup)

½ teaspoon ground fennel seeds

I 28-ounce can plum tomatoes with juice

2 cups chicken stock or water

2 teaspoons honey

Kosher salt and freshly ground black pepper

Fresh dill, for garnish

CUCUMBER-DILL YOGURT

½ cup 2% or whole milk Greek yogurt

½ cup finely diced seedless cucumber

I tablespoon chopped fresh chives

I tablespoon chopped fresh dill

I tablespoon extra-virgin olive oil

Kosher salt and freshly ground black pepper

1 To make the soup: In a large saucepan, heat the oil over medium heat. When the oil is hot, add the onion and carrot. Cook, stirring occasionally, until the onion is softened, 6 to 7 minutes.

2 Add the orange zest, orange juice, and ground fennel. Cook until fragrant, about 1 minute. Add the tomatoes and their juice, stock, honey, and 1 cup water. Season with salt and pepper. Bring to a simmer and cook, breaking up the tomatoes with a wooden spoon, until the tomatoes are very soft, about 40 minutes.

3 Make the cucumber-dill yogurt: In a small bowl, stir together the yogurt, cucumber, chives, dill, and oil. Season with salt and pepper and chill until ready to serve.

4 When the soup is finished, puree with a hand blender or in batches in a countertop blender. Refrigerate until chilled.

5 Serve in chilled soup bowls with a dollop of the cucumber-dill yogurt and a sprinkle of fresh dill sprigs.

45 TUNA
CANNED IN OLIVE OIL

Canned tuna is the best-selling "seafood" in America. Many brands and varieties are available, but I prefer Italian tuna canned in olive oil. The Italians take their tuna very seriously and some of the world's best tuna is caught off the shores of Sicily. In Italy, the fish is cooked, allowed to marinate in olive oil, and then canned.

I am a huge fan of this pantry staple, preferring it much more than fresh tuna. Keep an eye out for premium canned tuna in glass jars from Spain and Italy. It is more expensive but a great treat once in a while. I try to stock Ortiz at home and in my restaurants, and I eat canned tuna myself two or three times a week.

Tips

■ Don't automatically throw away the oil that the tuna has been packed in. Let taste be your guide. Try it and if it's not too fishy, use as some or all of the oil in the recipes, though don't cook with it: Because the smoke point has been lowered by the canning process, it could burn easily.

■ Canned tuna will keep for a long time in the pantry; just check the expiration date.

■ For a quick lunch, mix a can of tuna with whatever chopped vegetables you have in the fridge (carrots, cucumbers, onions, parsley, or olives all work nicely). I add grated Pecorino Romano cheese, and then make a simple dressing with red wine vinegar, lemon juice, and olive oil, and toss all together.

TUNA AIOLI DIP WITH BALSAMIC DRIZZLE

This is my take on the Italian classic tonnato sauce, traditionally a "thin" sauce for cold poached veal. Here I make it a little thicker, drizzle it with a reduced balsamic syrup to add another level of flavor, and serve it with crunchy fresh vegetables. ■ **SERVES 4 TO 6**

¼ cup balsamic vinegar

1 dried bay leaf

1 sprig fresh rosemary

1 6-ounce can tuna in olive oil, drained, reserving 2 tablespoons oil

⅓ cup mayonnaise

2 tablespoons capers, drained

2 anchovies

Juice of ½ lemon (about 1½ tablespoons)

Raw vegetables, such as carrots, celery, cucumber spears, endive leaves, sliced fennel, and bell pepper strips, for dipping

1 In a small saucepan, combine the vinegar, bay leaf, and rosemary. Bring to a boil and reduce until syrupy, about 1 tablespoon. Be careful—this happens quickly and can burn easily at the end. Let cool slightly while you make the dip and discard the bay leaf and rosemary sprig.

2 In a food processor, combine the tuna and reserved oil, the mayonnaise, capers, anchovies, and lemon juice. Process to make a smooth dip. Transfer to a flat serving bowl (you want a larger surface area to drizzle with the balsamic). Drizzle with the balsamic syrup and serve surrounded by crudités.

SALADE
NIÇOISE

TUNA AIOLI DIP
WITH BALSAMIC
DRIZZLE

TUNA SALAD
SANDWICH

SALADE NIÇOISE

This is my all-time favorite salad. It is a perfect marriage of protein, fresh vegetables, and vinaigrette. The trick to an excellent traditional Niçoise is to use premium canned tuna, for the most flavor and depth. ▪ **SERVES 4**

4 new red potatoes (about 12 ounces)

Kosher salt

4 ounces haricots verts, trimmed

¼ cup red wine vinegar

1 tablespoon Dijon mustard

Freshly ground black pepper

½ cup extra-virgin olive oil

10 cups torn Boston or other tender leaf lettuce, washed and dried

1½ cups cored, seeded, and diced tomato or halved cherry tomatoes

2 6-ounce cans tuna in olive oil, drained

3 hard-boiled eggs, peeled and quartered

8 anchovy fillets

½ cup Niçoise olives

1 Put the potatoes in a saucepan with water to cover by 1 inch. Bring to a simmer and cook until tender throughout, about 15 minutes. Drain and let cool slightly.

2 Meanwhile, bring a medium saucepan of salted water to a boil and add the haricots verts. Blanch until just tender, about 3 minutes. Cool under running water, drain, and pat dry.

3 In a medium bowl, whisk together the vinegar and mustard. Season with salt and pepper. Whisk in the oil in a slow, steady stream to make a smooth, emulsified vinaigrette.

4 Slice the warm potatoes and then toss in a medium bowl with a few tablespoons of the dressing. Season with salt and pepper.

5 Line a serving platter with the lettuce. Mound the potatoes on the lettuce. Toss the haricots verts with a few tablespoons of dressing, season with salt and pepper, and mound next to the potatoes. Repeat with the tomatoes and tuna, dressing separately and placing on the lettuce. Add the egg quarters, but don't toss with the dressing. Arrange the anchovies between the mounds of ingredients and scatter the olives. Drizzle a little more of the dressing over everything and serve family style, with any extra dressing on the side.

TUNA SALAD SANDWICH

Soft bread is essential and substituting challah for classic white bread elevates the sandwich but still allows that comforting kitchen table feel. Serve with chips and a pickle. ■ **MAKES 2 GENEROUS SANDWICHES**

2 6-ounce cans tuna in olive oil, drained

¼ cup finely diced celery

¼ cup finely diced red onion

⅓ cup mayonnaise

1 tablespoon Dijon mustard

2 teaspoons drained and chopped capers

Juice of ½ lemon (about 1½ tablespoons)

Kosher salt and freshly ground black pepper

4 slices challah or other soft egg bread

4 thick slices tomato, seasoned with salt and pepper

Red leaf lettuce, washed and dried

1 Put the tuna in a medium bowl and break up the large chunks with a fork. Stir in the celery and onion. Add the mayonnaise, mustard, capers, and lemon juice. Mix to thoroughly combine and coat all of the tuna with the dressing. Don't leave any big chunks of tuna. Season with salt and pepper and chill at least 30 minutes to let the flavors develop.

2 When ready to serve, lightly toast the challah. Divide the tuna between 2 slices of the challah and top both with the tomato slices and the lettuce. Top with the remaining slices of bread and serve.

VINEGAR
CIDER

Vinegar is a sour liquid made from the fermentation of ethanol (ethyl alcohol), typically wine. In the case of cider vinegar, it is made from pressed apples that are allowed to ferment into cider, then vinegar, and has a mellow taste with a hint of sweetness. It generally has an acidity level of 5 to 6 percent, putting it on par with most wine vinegars.

Cider vinegar is sometimes sold at health food stores unpasteurized and unfiltered with the "mother," a cloudy formation at the bottom, still in the bottle. These vinegars often have a more distinctive flavor than commercially produced cider vinegar.

Tips

- Vinegar lasts indefinitely and is best stored in a cool, dry place, away from light.

- If your vinegar develops sediment or a "mother" or becomes cloudy from age, it is still fine to use.

PORK ADOBO WITH COCONUT

I was inspired to create this recipe by a dear Filipina friend who would make her traditional version for our family each time our home was blessed with a new baby. Here, I change up the classic rendition by using coconut milk, ginger for floral heat, and cider vinegar instead of white vinegar. I serve it alongside simple long-grain white rice. ∎ **SERVES 4**

½ cup cider vinegar

½ cup soy sauce

2 tablespoons (packed) light brown sugar

4 garlic cloves, crushed

½ teaspoon coarsely ground black pepper

2 dried bay leaves

8 thick, meaty country-style pork ribs (3½ to 4 pounds total)

2 tablespoons canola oil

1 large onion, thickly sliced

2 garlic cloves, chopped

2 tablespoons finely chopped peeled fresh ginger

1 cup coconut milk

1 In a nonreactive baking dish just large enough to hold the ribs, whisk together the vinegar, soy sauce, sugar, crushed garlic, black pepper, and bay leaves. Add the pork and turn to coat in the marinade. Cover with plastic wrap and marinate in the refrigerator overnight or at least 4 hours.

2 Remove the ribs and strain the marinade, discarding the solids and bay leaves. In a large Dutch oven, heat 1 tablespoon of the oil over medium heat. When the oil is hot, add the onion, chopped garlic, and ginger and cook until the onion begins to soften, about 5 minutes. Add the pork, strained marinade, and 1 cup water. Bring to a simmer. Cover and simmer until the ribs are very tender, but not falling apart, about 1 hour.

3 Remove the ribs from the sauce and pat dry. In a large skillet, heat the remaining 1 tablespoon oil over medium-high heat. Return the adobo sauce to a gentle simmer and add the coconut milk. Sear the ribs in the skillet, just to caramelize all sides, about 1 minute per side. As the ribs are seared, return them to the adobo sauce. Once all the ribs are back in the sauce, return everything to a simmer and serve.

CHICKEN VINEGAR WITH CINNAMON CANDY

This is adapted from a recipe I came up with while competing on the Food Network's *The Next Iron Chef*. The cider vinegar perfectly opposes the sweet flavors of the candy, balsamic, and raisins, allowing all the various elements to come together. The cinnamon candy—the secret ingredient—was tough to incorporate, but I put to use my strong belief that almost anything can work in a dish as long as it is balanced correctly. ■ **SERVES 4 TO 6**

3 pounds small bone-in, skin-on chicken thighs

Kosher salt

2 tablespoons extra-virgin olive oil

1 slice bacon, finely chopped

2 medium shallots, finely chopped

3 garlic cloves, finely chopped

1 tablespoon finely chopped peeled fresh ginger

½ cup balsamic vinegar

½ cup cider vinegar

3 ripe plum tomatoes, cored, seeded, and chopped (about 1½ cups)

1 cup chicken stock

2 tablespoons golden raisins

1 tablespoon hard cinnamon candies, tied in cheesecloth

2 tablespoons (¼ stick) unsalted butter, cut into pieces

2 tablespoons chopped fresh Italian parsley

1 Pat the chicken very dry and season with salt. Heat a large shallow Dutch oven over medium-high heat. Add the oil. When the oil is hot, add the chicken, skin side down, and cook until the skin is crisp and golden, 4 to 5 minutes. Turn and brown the other side, about 2 minutes more. Remove the chicken to a plate.

2 Reduce the heat to medium and add the bacon. Cook and stir until the bacon renders its fat and crisps, about 2 minutes. Add the shallots, garlic, and ginger and cook until the shallots are wilted, about 3 minutes.

3 Pour in both vinegars, raise the heat to high, and cook until reduced by half, about 3 minutes. Add the tomatoes, chicken stock, raisins, and candies. Adjust the heat so the sauce simmers and then add the chicken, skin side up. Cover and cook until the chicken is tender, 20 to 25 minutes.

4 Uncover and simmer rapidly for 5 minutes to thicken the sauce. Discard the cinnamon candies. Remove the chicken and arrange on a serving platter. Whisk the butter into the sauce, pour over the chicken, sprinkle with the parsley, and serve.

**CHICKEN VINEGAR
WITH CINNAMON CANDY**

**APPLE CIDER
DOUGHNUTS
WITH CIDER
VINEGAR GLAZE**

**PORK ADOBO
WITH COCONUT**

APPLE CIDER DOUGHNUTS
WITH CIDER VINEGAR GLAZE

I use cider vinegar in two ways here, first in the batter, to make a quick version of homemade buttermilk by curdling regular whole milk with cider vinegar. It turns up again as a tart accent in the confectioners' sugar glaze.

■ **MAKES I BAKER'S DOZEN, PLUS DOUGHNUT HOLES**

DOUGHNUTS

I cup apple cider

½ cup whole milk

2 teaspoons cider vinegar

4 cups all-purpose flour, plus more for rolling

2 teaspoons baking powder

I teaspoon baking soda

½ teaspoon ground cinnamon

½ teaspoon kosher salt

¼ teaspoon freshly grated nutmeg

I cup sugar

¼ cup shortening

2 large eggs

I teaspoon pure vanilla extract

Canola oil, for frying

GLAZE

2 cups confectioners' sugar, sifted

2 tablespoons cider vinegar

I teaspoon pure vanilla extract

1 To make the doughnuts: Bring the apple cider to a boil in a small saucepan and reduce to ½ cup, 3 to 4 minutes. Let cool.

2 In a liquid measuring cup, combine the milk and vinegar. Let sit 5 minutes to curdle into buttermilk, and stir. Sift together the flour, baking powder, baking soda, cinnamon, salt, and nutmeg.

3 In the bowl of an electric mixer fitted with the paddle attachment, cream the sugar and shortening together on high speed for 1 minute. Reduce the speed to medium and add the eggs, 1 at a time, until incorporated, then mix in the vanilla. Add the buttermilk and cooled cider and mix until combined. Add the sifted flour mixture and mix on low just until a dough comes together. Chill the dough 30 minutes in the refrigerator.

4 When ready to fry, heat 2 inches of oil in a deep pot to 365°F. Roll half the dough on a floured work surface to about ¾-inch thickness. Cut as many doughnuts as you can with a 3½- to 4-inch cutter. Use a 1-inch cutter, or slightly smaller, to make the doughnut holes. You should get 6 or 7 doughnuts from each half of the dough. Chill the first half of the doughnuts in the refrigerator while you roll out the second half.

5 To make the glaze: In a small bowl, whisk together the confectioners' sugar, vinegar, vanilla, and 1 tablespoon water to make a thick glaze. You should be able to drizzle the glaze from a spoon. If it's too thick, add a little more water.

6 Fry the doughnuts in 2 batches until dark golden brown, about 2 minutes per side (a little less for the doughnut holes). Drain on paper towels and bring the oil back to 365°F. before frying the second batch. While the doughnuts are still warm, dip the surface of one side in the glaze. Let the glaze set with the glazed side up on a cooling rack for 5 to 10 minutes. These doughnuts are best served warm or at least within 1 or 2 hours of frying.

47 VINEGAR
RED WINE

The accidental discovery in ancient times that the juice of grapes would eventually turn to wine was a revelation. The further discovery that wine, left to its own devices, would eventually become vinegar probably was not cause for such immediate celebration. Vinegar, though, has proven useful in so many ways—as a cleanser, preservative, and, of course, cooking ingredient in nearly every type of cuisine.

As with the wine we drink, there is a huge range in quality for wine vinegars. The better wine vinegars are aged in wood for up to two years and have a more complex, mellow flavor than commercial wine vinegars. The best and most interesting vinegars are made from individual varieties of grapes, as opposed to a mass quantity of leftover grapes. I like a Cabernet red wine vinegar, but you can try a few and see which one you prefer.

Tips

- Always choose a quality brand and purchase in small quantities.

- As a good rule of thumb, pair your vinegar with food as you would wine. Use red wine vinegar to go along with hearty meals.

SIMPLE GARDEN LETTUCE SALAD
WITH RED WINE VINAIGRETTE

This is a vinaigrette at its most classic and basic. Here I use fresh garden lettuce (could be from your farmers' market) and fresh soft herbs to make a delicate spring salad. Once you master this dressing, you will think of countless uses for it all year long. Use only as much dressing as you need to lightly coat the lettuce. If there is any left over, it will keep in the refrigerator for three or four days. You can use leftover glass Dijon mustard jars as vessels to build and then shake the dressing in. ■ SERVES 4

2 teaspoons very finely chopped shallot

2 tablespoons red wine vinegar

Kosher salt and freshly ground black pepper

2 teaspoons Dijon mustard

6 tablespoons extra-virgin olive oil

16 cups loosely packed garden leaf lettuce, washed and dried

1½ cups snipped fresh soft herbs, such as any combination of parsley, chives, dill, basil, chervil, and tarragon

1 In a medium bowl, combine the shallot and vinegar. Season with salt and pepper. Let sit for 10 minutes to infuse the vinegar with the shallot flavor.

2 Whisk the mustard into the vinegar. Whisk in the oil in a slow, steady stream to make a smooth and emulsified dressing.

3 Put the lettuce and herbs in a large serving bowl. Drizzle with about half the dressing and season lightly with salt and pepper. Toss to coat the salad with the dressing, adding more dressing as needed. Serve immediately.

WARM WILD MUSHROOMS

AVOCADO AND GRAPEFRUIT SALAD

SIMPLE GARDEN LETTUCE SALAD WITH RED WINE VINAIGRETTE

AVOCADO AND GRAPEFRUIT SALAD

The grapefruit juice alone does not have enough acidity to make a well-balanced dressing, so I add a little red wine vinegar to pull it all together. This is a terrific first course, especially before a hearty stew or soup.

■ **SERVES 4 TO 6**

½ small red onion, thinly sliced

2 large pink grapefruits

2 tablespoons red wine vinegar

1 teaspoon honey

Kosher salt and freshly ground black pepper

6 tablespoons extra-virgin olive oil

2 ripe avocados, pitted, peeled, and cubed

2 bunches watercress, tough stems trimmed, then washed and dried

1 Fill a small bowl with ice water and add the onion. While you prepare the salad, let the onion soak, to remove some of the bite and crisp it up.

2 With a serrated knife, trim the ends from 1 grapefruit so it sits flat on your cutting board. Slice off the peel and pith in a downward motion, leaving just the flesh and membranes. Hold the grapefruit in your hand and cut out the grapefruit segments into a small bowl, until only the membrane remains. Repeat with the remaining grapefruit. Squeeze any extra juice from the membranes into a large bowl.

3 Whisk the vinegar and honey into the large bowl with the juice. Season with salt and pepper. Whisk in the oil in a slow, steady stream to make a smooth dressing. Add the grapefruit segments, avocados, and watercress. Drain the onion, pat dry, and add. Toss gently to coat with the dressing, adjust the seasoning, and serve.

WARM WILD MUSHROOMS

Red wine and wild mushrooms are a classic combination. The red wine vinegar gives these mushrooms a bright flavor that you would not get from just adding wine. Any leftover mushrooms can be stirred into polenta or rice, used as a topping for scrambled eggs or grilled steak, or added to a sandwich. ■ SERVES 4 TO 6

2 tablespoons extra-virgin olive oil, plus more as necessary

2 pounds mixed wild mushrooms, such as any combination of cremini, shiitake, chanterelle, oyster, and porcini, thickly sliced

1 medium shallot, finely chopped

1 tablespoon chopped fresh tarragon

2 tablespoons red wine vinegar

2 tablespoons chopped fresh Italian parsley

Kosher salt

3 tablespoons unsalted butter, cut into pieces

12 slices toasted baguette

1 In a large skillet over medium-high heat, add the oil, and when it is hot, add enough mushrooms just to cover the bottom of the pan (ultimately, you'll probably cook the mushrooms in 2 batches). Cook the mushrooms without stirring until browned on 1 side and then turn the mushrooms. Continue cooking, stirring occasionally, until the mushrooms are well browned on both sides, about 5 minutes. Remove to a plate and repeat with the remaining mushrooms, adding a little more oil to the pan if necessary.

2 Scrape the mushrooms back into the pan. Over medium heat, add the shallot and sauté until tender, about 5 minutes. Add the tarragon and vinegar and cook until the mushrooms absorb the vinegar. Sprinkle with the parsley and season with salt. Add the butter pieces and swirl the pan until the butter melts and forms a sauce. Serve immediately over the baguette slices.

VINEGAR
WHITE WINE

White wine vinegar is produced in exactly the same way as red wine vinegar, and its quality is also affected by how long it has been aged and which grape varietals were used. For the best quality, look for small-batch, aged vinegars made from a single variety of grape. I prefer white wine vinegar made from Chardonnay. As with red wine vinegar, pair your white wine vinegar with your food as you would your white wine. White wine vinegar goes well with light or brighter meals.

Tips

- Always choose a quality brand and purchase in small quantities.

- Inexpensive vinegars are not a good choice for salads. Spend a few dollars more and you will notice the difference in the simplest of vinaigrettes.

CRAB BRUSCHETTA
WITH CUCUMBER CHILE MIGNONETTE

Mignonette is a classic French accompaniment to raw oysters on the half shell. It is made of white wine vinegar, shallots, and lots of black pepper. Here I trade the black pepper for the fresher taste of a raw fresno chile and use the sauce to dress the crab. You can also toss the mignonette with greens, poached shrimp, or calamari and a little more oil and vinegar for a quick seafood salad. ■ **MAKES 1 DOZEN BRUSCHETTA**

CUCUMBER CHILE MIGNONETTE

1 cup diced English cucumber

1 small shallot, finely diced, about 2 tablespoons

1 small fresno chile pepper, seeded and finely chopped, about 2 teaspoons

¼ cup white wine vinegar

Pinch of sugar

Kosher salt

CRAB SALAD

8 ounces lump crabmeat, picked through for shells

2 tablespoons chopped fresh mint

12 slices lightly toasted baguette

1 To make the cucumber chile mignonette: In a medium bowl, stir together the cucumber, shallot, and chile pepper. Stir in the vinegar and season with a pinch of sugar and a little salt. Refrigerate until well chilled, about 30 minutes.

2 To make the crab: When ready to serve, place the crabmeat in a medium bowl. Drizzle with about three quarters of the mignonette, add the mint, and toss. Arrange the baguette slices on a serving tray and top with the crab. Drizzle the remaining mignonette on top of each bruschetta.

SPINACH SALAD WITH TOMATO VINAIGRETTE

CRAB BRUSCHETTA WITH CUCUMBER CHILE MIGNONETTE

SNAP PEA AND PARMIGIANO-REGGIANO SALAD

SNAP PEA AND PARMIGIANO-REGGIANO SALAD

I think white wine vinegar has a more delicate flavor than red or cider vinegar, which makes it the right choice for this light spring salad. It is also virtually colorless, which helps to preserve the bright hues of your ingredients. ■ **SERVES 4 TO 6**

Kosher salt

1 pound sugar snap peas, strings removed

2 tablespoons white wine vinegar

1 teaspoon Dijon mustard

⅓ cup extra-virgin olive oil

Freshly ground black pepper

1 cup julienned radishes

½ cup fresh Italian parsley leaves

½ cup fresh mint leaves, roughly torn if large

½ cup shaved Parmigiano-Reggiano (use a vegetable peeler for long shavings)

1 Bring a large pot of salted water to a boil. Add the snap peas and cook until crisp-tender, 2 to 3 minutes. Drain and immediately plunge into a bowl of ice water and cool completely. Drain and pat dry.

2 In a large serving bowl, whisk together the vinegar and mustard. Whisk in the oil in a slow, steady stream to make a smooth and emulsified dressing. Season with salt and pepper.

3 To the dressing, add the snap peas, radishes, parsley, and mint. Toss well to coat the vegetables with the dressing. Add the cheese shavings and toss lightly, taking care not to break up the shavings.

SPINACH SALAD WITH TOMATO VINAIGRETTE

In this vinaigrette, the tomato adds sweetness, acidity, and body, so I can use more vinegar and less oil and still get the same result as the traditional ratio for classic vinaigrettes (which is three parts oil to one part vinegar). The dressing can be made ahead and will keep for one or two days in the refrigerator. ■ SERVES 4

1 medium plum tomato, cored, seeded, and cut into chunks

¼ cup white wine vinegar

1 teaspoon honey

¼ cup extra-virgin olive oil

Kosher salt

8 cups baby spinach

1½ cups cherry tomatoes, halved if large

4 slices cooked bacon, crumbled

¼ cup sliced red onion

1 avocado, pitted, peeled, and diced

Freshly ground black pepper

1 In a blender, combine the plum tomato, vinegar, and honey. Puree until smooth. With the blender running, pour the oil in through the top in a slow and steady stream to make a smooth, thick dressing. Season with salt.

2 In a serving bowl, combine the spinach, cherry tomatoes, bacon, onion, and avocado. Drizzle with the dressing, season with salt and pepper, and toss well. Serve immediately.

49 WORCESTERSHIRE SAUCE

Created by Lea & Perrins in 1835, Worcestershire sauce ingeniously combines a profile of varied flavors such as anchovy, tamarind, clove, vinegar, garlic, onion, molasses, and some other "secret stuff" that has never been divulged. The concoction is barrel-aged for over a year and then diluted with water to cut the knock-you-out quality it has before it is bottled.

Sweet. Acidic. Salty. Maddeningly delicious. It is a one-of-a-kind, highly versatile invention that lends depth to sauces and marinades for beef, pork, poultry, and lamb; and it is simply wonderful as a condiment all on its own. Sometimes, I even dash it across my over-easy eggs in the morning. I think this is one of the best sauces to have ever been bottled. I never, ever leave my pantry vacant of Worcestershire sauce.

Tips

- Once opened, Worcestershire sauce will keep up to 1 year in the fridge, but it is best used within a few months to maintain that punch of flavor.

- Worcestershire sauce is a great quick marinade for burgers. Just shake the sauce on a plate and dredge the burgers on both sides. Let sit while you preheat your grill.

THE BLOODY MARY

A true Bloody Mary cannot exist without Worcestershire sauce. It is one of the essential ingredients lending those hard-to-discern flavor undertones in the drink. The Bloody Mary mix can be made a day or two ahead of time— just stir before mixing with the vodka. ■ **MAKES 1 QUART OF MIX, 4 TO 6 COCKTAILS**

1 quart 100% vegetable juice, preferably V-8

1 teaspoon celery salt

Freshly ground black pepper

Juice of 1 lime (about 2 tablespoons)

Juice of ½ lemon (about 1½ tablespoons)

2 tablespoons prepared horseradish, drained

2 tablespoons whole grain Dijon mustard

2 dashes green Tabasco sauce

1 tablespoon Worcestershire sauce

Vodka

Cucumber spears and lemon wedges, for garnish

1 To a large glass pitcher, add the vegetable juice, celery salt, pepper, lime juice, lemon juice, horseradish, mustard, Tabasco, and Worcestershire. Stir thoroughly, but don't shake.

2 For 1 Bloody Mary, fill a highball glass with ice. Add 2 ounces (¼ cup) of vodka. Fill the glass with the Bloody Mary mixture. Garnish with a spear of cucumber and a wedge of lemon.

FOOLPROOF BBQ SAUCE

This is a versatile BBQ sauce—great on beef ribs, pork, and poultry. This recipe makes a big batch of sauce, but it will keep for a week in the fridge and it also freezes well. For recipes that use BBQ sauce, see Supercharged Chicken Wings (page 45), Cast-Iron Burgers with Secret Sauce (page 46), and Marinated Flank Steak with Mashed Sweet Potatoes (page 42).

■ **MAKES 2 QUARTS**

1 tablespoon canola oil

3 medium white onions, finely chopped (about 5 cups)

3 garlic cloves, finely chopped

½ cup raisins

1 teaspoon ground cumin

8 ounces tomato paste (about 1 cup)

4 canned chipotle peppers in adobo sauce, chopped, plus 2 tablespoons adobo sauce (about ⅓ cup)

1 tablespoon anchovy paste

1 quart unseasoned chicken stock

1 cup cider vinegar

1 cup honey

½ cup orange juice concentrate, thawed

½ cup Dijon mustard

½ cup molasses

1 tablespoon fish sauce

¼ cup Worcestershire sauce, plus 2 tablespoons to finish

Kosher salt and freshly ground black pepper

1 In a medium Dutch oven over low heat, heat the oil. When the oil is hot, add the onions and garlic, slowly sweating them until tender but not colored, about 20 minutes. Add the raisins, cumin, tomato paste, chipotles, and anchovy paste. Sweat over low heat another 5 minutes, taking care not to scorch.

2 Add the stock, vinegar, honey, orange juice concentrate, mustard, molasses, fish sauce, and ¼ cup of the Worcestershire. Simmer over low heat until thick and silky, 50 to 60 minutes. You can puree the sauce with a hand blender to incorporate the raisins, if you like, but I just leave them as is; I like the chewy flavor. Adjust the seasoning with salt and pepper. Stir in the remaining 2 tablespoons Worcestershire.

FOOLPROOF BBQ SAUCE

GRILLED LAMB WITH WORCESTERSHIRE AND WATERCRESS

THE BLOODY MARY

GRILLED LAMB
WITH WORCESTERSHIRE AND WATERCRESS

The savoriness of Worcestershire and the bitterness of the watercress pair well with the slight gaminess of the lamb. To feed a larger crowd, you could serve this same condiment with a grilled butterflied leg of lamb. ■ SERVES 4

4 cups loosely packed watercress, washed and dried

$\frac{1}{2}$ cup loosely packed fresh tarragon leaves

2 garlic cloves, finely chopped

$\frac{1}{4}$ cup red wine vinegar

2 tablespoons capers, drained

1 tablespoon Dijon mustard

1 tablespoon Worcestershire sauce

4 white anchovies packed in vinegar

$\frac{1}{2}$ cup extra-virgin olive oil

2 hard-boiled eggs, finely chopped

Kosher salt and freshly ground black pepper

8 lamb rib chops (2$\frac{1}{2}$ pounds total and 1$\frac{1}{2}$ inches thick), Frenched

1 In a food processor, combine the watercress, tarragon, garlic, vinegar, capers, mustard, Worcestershire, and anchovies. Pulse to combine. With the machine running, pour in the oil to make a chunky sauce. It should be rough and salsalike, not too smooth. Transfer the sauce to a nonreactive bowl. Fold in the eggs. Season with salt and pepper.

2 Heat a grill pan over medium-high heat. Season the lamb chops liberally with salt and pepper and grill on both sides until medium rare, about 4 minutes per side. Arrange on a platter family style, spoon the watercress condiment on top, and serve.

YEAST

Yeast is a living single-celled organism. A yeast cell may be tiny, but many of them together, in the right growing conditions, create quite a reaction. The by-products of their growth include carbon dioxide (to help dough rise) and alcohol (for flavor and that unmistakable yeasty scent of baking bread).

Wild yeasts are in the air at all times, but "domesticated" yeast is what we buy at the store. It is all basically the same strain of yeast, which makes it remarkably consistent. The main types of yeast you will see in stores are active dry, instant or rapid-rise, and cake yeast. Active dry is the most reliable of the three and is what I use. It is a combination of dead yeast cells surrounding a smaller number of live cells, so it must be "activated" (dissolved in warm water) before use.

Tips

- I package active dry yeast = 2¼ teaspoons yeast

- Unopened packages of yeast will keep in the refrigerator for several weeks or the freezer for longer-term storage. Opened packages should be put inside a resealable plastic bag and can be stored the same way. It is crucial that the yeast not be exposed to moisture.

- Do not be tempted to buy "rapid-rise" yeast. It works fast, but the cells also die much faster and don't have enough time to develop any flavor.

GRAPE AND OLIVE FLATBREAD

I used to keep this family favorite reserved for the children, but now, I love to prepare and bake it in front of guests when they just arrive. The aroma of the rosemary and grapes coming out of the oven fills the kitchen and draws everyone in. You can cut the flatbread in a variety of ways—I like triangle slices or small rectangles so they are perfectly suited for an easily eaten hors d'oeuvre. ■ **MAKES 4 INDIVIDUAL FLATBREADS**

DOUGH

I teaspoon active dry yeast

1½ cups warm water (about 100°F., or just warm to the touch)

Pinch of sugar

3 tablespoons extra-virgin olive oil, plus more for the bowl

2 teaspoons kosher salt

3 to 3½ cups all-purpose flour, plus more for shaping the dough

FLATBREAD

1½ cups small seedless red grapes, halved

½ cup pitted and halved Kalamata olives

1 tablespoon chopped fresh rosemary

2 tablespoons extra-virgin olive oil

Kosher salt

1 To make the dough: Prepare the dough the day before making the flatbreads. In a spouted measuring cup, mix the yeast with ½ cup of the warm water and the sugar. Let proof at room temperature until a little bubbly, about 5 minutes.

2 In another measuring cup, mix the oil and salt with the remaining 1 cup warm water, stirring until the salt dissolves. Put 3 cups flour in the bowl of an electric mixer fitted with the paddle attachment and pour in both water mixtures. Beat on medium speed until the dough comes together (you don't want a ball to form at this point; the dough should still be a little sticky). Add more flour or water, if necessary. Switch to the dough hook and mix on medium high until the dough is a soft, supple ball, about 2 minutes. Knead the dough on a floured countertop a few times. Coat a large bowl with oil and turn the dough to coat in the oil. Cover lightly with plastic wrap or a kitchen towel and let rise until doubled, about 1 hour. Punch down the dough and then put it in an oiled zip-top bag and press out any excess air. Let it proof in the fridge overnight or as long as 1 day.

3 When you are ready to make the flatbread: Let the dough come to room temperature and preheat the oven to 450°F., with a pizza stone (or flat baking sheet) on the bottom rack. In a bowl, toss the grapes, olives, and rosemary with the oil and season with salt.

4 Divide the dough into 4 pieces and then roll into loose balls and flatten into four 8- to 9-inch rounds. Place 1 round of dough on a parchment-paper-lined pizza peel or overturned sheet pan (the parchment will make it easier to slide the dough onto the stone). Scatter one quarter of the grape-olive mixture on the dough. Slide the round onto the pizza stone and bake until browned and the dough is cooked through, about 10 minutes. Repeat with the remaining 3 dough rounds and the toppings. Cut into wedges and serve warm or at room temperature.

CARAMELIZED
ONION TART

CHICKEN POT PIE

GRAPE AND OLIVE
FLATBREAD

CHICKEN POT PIE

Instead of a heavier traditional biscuit dough, I use a twist on "angel biscuits," a light airy biscuit that untraditionally uses yeast in the dough. This recipe makes four individual pot pies, but you can also make one large pot pie in an eight-inch rectangular or square baking dish. Simply cut the biscuits to fill in the top of the baking dish and bake for an extra 5 minutes.

■ SERVES 4

BISCUITS

1 teaspoon active dry yeast

¼ cup lukewarm water (about 100°F., or just warm to the touch)

2½ cups all-purpose flour, plus extra for rolling

1 teaspoon sugar

1½ teaspoons baking powder

½ teaspoon baking soda

½ teaspoon kosher salt

6 tablespoons (¾ stick) unsalted butter, chilled and cut into pieces

1 cup chilled buttermilk

FILLING

3 tablespoons unsalted butter

2 small leeks (white and light green parts), chopped (about 1 cup)

2 medium carrots, chopped (about 2 cups)

4 ounces button mushrooms, sliced (about 2 cups)

1 tablespoon chopped fresh thyme

1 tablespoon chopped fresh tarragon

3 tablespoons all-purpose flour

3 cups chicken stock

2½ cups cubed or shredded cooked boneless, skinless chicken

⅓ cup heavy cream, plus more for brushing

1 cup frozen peas, thawed

Juice of ½ lemon, or to taste

1 To make the biscuits: Preheat the oven to 425°F. In a spouted measuring cup, stir together the yeast and warm water to dissolve. Let sit 5 minutes, until a little bubbly.

2 In a food processor, combine the flour, sugar, baking powder, baking soda, and salt. Pulse to combine. Add the butter and pulse until the butter is dispersed and about the size of small peas. With the machine running, pour in the buttermilk and process just until the mixture comes together in a shaggy dough.

3 Dump the dough onto a floured countertop and knead once or twice until it comes together. Roll into a square about ¾ inch thick. Using a large biscuit cutter, cut 4 or 5 biscuits to fit your baking vessels (I used 1½-cup ramekins with a 4-inch diameter). Transfer the biscuits to a floured baking sheet, cover lightly with plastic wrap, and let rise while you make the filling, about 30 minutes.

4 To make the filling: In a large skillet over medium heat, melt the butter. When melted, add the leeks, carrots, and mushrooms and cook until wilted, about 7 minutes.

5 Stir in the thyme and tarragon and then sprinkle the flour all over. Stir to coat the vegetables with the flour and cook until the flour smells toasted (but is not browned), 2 to 3 minutes. Pour in the stock and bring to a simmer. Cook until the vegetables are tender, about 10 minutes. Stir in the chicken, cream, and peas and simmer until the peas are just heated through, about 3 minutes. Stir in lemon juice (you don't want the filling to taste lemony; the lemon juice just serves to brighten the other flavors in the sauce).

6 Pour the filling into the individual ramekins and gently fit 1 biscuit on top of each. Brush lightly with cream. Bake until the filling is bubbly and the biscuits are deep golden brown, about 18 minutes. Let cool 5 minutes before serving.

CARAMELIZED ONION TART

The active dry yeast produces a hearty dough that holds up well to the savory nature of this dish. The natural sugars in the cooked onions impart a sweet balance to the sherry, thyme, and custard. ▪ **SERVES 6 TO 8**

DOUGH

1 teaspoon active dry yeast

Pinch of sugar

¼ cup warm water (about 100°F., or just warm to the touch)

1⅓ cups all-purpose flour, plus more as needed

1 large egg

½ teaspoon kosher salt

2 tablespoons (¼ stick) unsalted butter, at room temperature, cut into pieces

Olive oil, for the bowl

FILLING

2 tablespoons (¼ stick) unsalted butter

2 pounds onions, sliced ¼ inch thick (about 8 cups)

½ teaspoon sugar

Kosher salt

1 tablespoon dry sherry

1 tablespoon chopped fresh thyme

2 large eggs

1 cup half-and-half

½ cup freshly grated Parmigiano-Reggiano

Cooking spray

1 To make the dough: In a spouted measuring cup, mix together the yeast and sugar in the water. Let proof until bubbly, about 5 minutes.

2 In the bowl of an electric mixer fitted with the paddle attachment, combine the flour, egg, salt, and yeast mixture. Mix on medium speed until combined. Increase the speed to medium high and add the butter, a few pieces at a time, until all is incorporated. Mix another 2 to 3 minutes on medium high to make a smooth but sticky dough. The dough will almost clean the sides of the bowl; add a few more tablespoons of flour, if necessary, to get to this point. Scrape the dough onto a floured work surface, knead once or twice, and transfer to an oiled bowl. Let rise at room temperature until doubled in bulk, about 1 hour.

3 While the dough rises, make the filling: In a large skillet over medium heat, add the butter. When melted, add the onions and sugar and season with salt. Cook, stirring occasionally, until the onions are deep golden brown and very soft, about 45 minutes. Add the sherry and thyme and cook until the sherry is absorbed, 1 to 2 minutes. Remove from the heat and allow the onions to cool to room temperature.

4 When you are ready to make the tart, preheat the oven to 350°F. In a large bowl, whisk together the eggs, half-and-half, and cheese and season with salt. Punch down the dough and on a floured work surface roll the dough into a 12-inch circle. Fit the dough into an 8- or 9-inch deep-dish pie plate sprayed with cooking spray and trim the dough so it is flush with the edge of the pie plate. Spread the cooled onions in the bottom and pour the custard over.

5 Bake until the tart is just set in the center and the crust is dark golden brown all over, about 40 minutes. Cool on a rack and serve warm or at room temperature.

A WORD OF THANKS

Truly, I am so proud to hold this book in my hands, and I know that it would never have been possible without the collaboration of many extraordinary minds. My sincere appreciation goes out to: Pam Krauss, Doris Cooper, Jim Massey, Ben Fink, Allison Renzulli, Amanda Englander, Sean Boyles, Kim Tyner, Jan Derevjanik, Janet McDonald, Sigi Nacson, Eric Lupfer, Scott Feldman, Jaret Keller, Tara Halper, Val Aikman-Smith, Chelsea Bawot, Nissa Quanstrom, Kassandra Medeiros, and Martha Tinkler.

In addition: My wife, Margaret, thank you for writing and researching and pouring your heart into my vision. Your detailed creativity shows on each and every page and your support is unparalleled. Amy Stevenson, the sheer depth of your knowledge and culinary skill impresses and amazes me at each turn. You were the perfect kitchen-mate and without your acumen the book simply would not have been the same. Emily Takoudes, you were this book's champion from the beginning, and you put your trust and faith in me wholeheartedly. Your passion and razor-sharp focus kept me on point every step of the way. Jane Treuhaft, I so enjoyed your perspective and eye for design. You refined my goal for the visuals and worked hard to bring it all to life. Sarah Remington, you were ready to run as soon as the light turned green. The photography is more than I could have imagined, and I anxiously await the next project we can work on together.

To my mother, Viola, in your day-to-day toil you unknowingly passed on to me a wealth of information, which I would be lost without. I remember our family meals each time I open my pantry door. Thank you for your tireless efforts and all those delicious meals.

INDEX